THE **W**ORD ON

# SEX, DRUGS

# & ROCK 'N' ROLL

# JIM BURNS

Gospel Light

Gospel Light, is an evangelical Christian publisher dedicated to serving the local church. We believe God's vision for Gospel Light is to provide church leaders with biblical, user-friendly materials that will help them evangelize, disciple and minister to children, youth and families.

We hope this Gospel Light resource will help you discover biblical truth for your own life and help you minister to youth. God bless you in your work.

*For a free catalog of resources from Gospel Light please contact your Christian supplier or call 1-800-4-GOSPEL.*

**PUBLISHING STAFF**
**Jean Daly,** Editor
**Kyle Duncan,** Editorial Director
**Gary S. Greig, Ph.D.,** Senior Editor
**Mary Gross,** Contributing Writer

ISBN 0-8307-1642-4
© 1994 Jim Burns
All rights reserved.
Printed in U.S.A.

# How to Make Clean Copies from This Book

### You may make copies of portions of this book with a clean conscience if:

• you (or someone in your organization) are the original purchaser;

• you are using the copies you make for a noncommercial purpose (such as teaching or promoting your ministry) within your church or organization;

• you follow the instructions provided in this book.

### However, it is ILLEGAL for you to make copies if:

• you are using the material to promote, advertise or sell a product or service other than for ministry fundraising;

• you are using the material in or on a product for sale;

• you or your organization are **not** the original purchaser of this book.

By following these guidelines you help us keep our products affordable. Thank you,

Gospel Light

# PRAISE FOR YOUTHBUILDERS

I deeply respect and appreciate the groundwork Jim Burns has prepared for true teenage discernment. *YouthBuilders* is timeless in the sense that the framework has made it possible to plug into any society, at any point in time, and to proceed to discuss, experience and arrive at sincere moral and Christian conclusions that will lead to growth and life changes. Reaching young people may be more difficult today than ever before, but God's grace is alive and well in Jim Burns and this wonderful curriculum.

**Fr. Angelo J. Artemas,** Youth Ministry Director, Greek Orthodox Archdiocese of North and South America

Jim Burns' work represents his integrity and intelligence, along with his heart for kids. *YouthBuilders* will change some lives and save many others.

**Stephen Arterburn,** Cofounder, The Minirth-Meier New Life Clinics

I heartily recommend Jim Burns' *Youth Builders Group Bible Studies* because they are leader-friendly tools that are ready-to-use in youth groups and Sunday School classes. Jim addresses the tough questions that students are genuinely facing every day and, through his engaging style, challenges young people to make their own decisions to move from their current opinions to God's convictions taught in the Bible. Every youth group will benefit from this excellent curriculum.

**Paul Borthwick,** Minister of Missions, Grace Chapel

It is about time that someone who knows kids, understands kids and works with kids writes youth curriculum that youth workers, both volunteer and professional, can use. Jim Burns' *YouthBuilders Group Bible Studies* is the curriculum that youth ministry has been waiting a long time for.

**Ridge Burns,** President, The Center for Student Missions

Jim Burns has found the right balance between learning God's Word and applying it to life. The topics are relevant, up-to-date and on target. Jim gets kids to think. The Parent Page is an extra bonus that continues the teaching in the home and helps involve parents in the process. This is a terrific series, and I highly recommend it.

**Les J. Christie,** Chair of Youth Ministries Department, San Jose Christian College

**T**here are very few people in the world who know how to communicate life-changing truth effectively to teens. Jim Burns is one of the best. *YouthBuilders Group Bible Studies* puts handles on those skills and makes them available to everyone. These studies are biblically sound, hands-on practical and just plain fun. This one gets a five-star endorsement—which isn't bad since there are only four stars to start with.

**Ken Davis,** President, Dynamic Communications

**I** don't know anyone who knows and understands the needs of the youth worker like Jim Burns. His new curriculum not only reveals his knowledge of youth ministry but also his depth and sensitivity to the Scriptures. *YouthBuilders Group Bible Studies* is solid, easy to use and gets students out of their seats and into the Word. I've been waiting for something like this for a long time!

**Doug Fields,** Pastor of High School, Saddleback Valley Community Church

**J**im Burns has a way of being creative without being "hokey." *YouthBuilders Group Bible Studies* take the age-old model of curriculum and gives it a new look with tools such as the Bible *Tuck-in*™ and Parent Page. Give this new resource a try and you'll see that Jim shoots straight forward on tough issues. The *YouthBuilders* series is great for leading small group discussions as well as teaching a large class of junior high or high school students. The Parent Page will help you get support from your parents in that they will understand the topics you are dealing with in your group. Put Jim's years of experience to work for you by equipping yourself with this quality material.

**Curt Gibson,** Pastor to Junior High, First Church of the Nazarene of Pasadena

**O**nce again, Jim Burns has managed to handle very timely issues with just the right touch. His *YouthBuilders Group Bible Studies* succeeds in teaching solid, biblical values without being stuffy or preachy. The format is user-friendly, designed to stimulate high involvement and deep discussion. Especially impressive is the Parent Page, a long overdue tool to help parents become part of the Christian education loop. I look forward to using it with my kids!

**David M. Hughes,** Pastor, First Baptist Church, Winston-Salem

**W**hat do you get when you combine a deep love for teens, over 20 years experience in youth ministry and an excellent writer? You get Jim Burns' *YouthBuilders* series! This stuff has absolutely hit the nail on the head. Quality Sunday School and small group material is tough to come by these days, but Jim has put every ounce of creativity he has into these books.

**Greg Johnson,** author of *Getting Ready for the Guy/Girl Thing* and *Keeping Your Cool While Sharing Your Faith*

**J**im Burns has a gift, the gift of combining the relational and theological dynamics of our faith in a graceful, relevant and easy-to-chew-and-swallow way. *YouthBuilders Group Bible Studies* are a hit, not only for teens but for teachers.

**Gregg Johnson,** National Youth Director, International Church of the Foursquare Gospel

continued on page 185

# DEDICATION

To Rik Mumma, Steve Arterburn and Bob Sharp.

Each in your own way have contributed more than you will ever imagine to my life and ministry.

"There is a friend who sticks closer than a brother" (Proverbs 18:24).

"As iron sharpens iron, so one man sharpens another" (Proverbs 27:17).

# **C** ONTENTS

# THANKS AND THANKS AGAIN!

This project is definitely a team effort. First of all, thank you to Cathy, Christy, Rebecca and Heidi Burns, the women of my life.

Thank you to Jill Corey, my incredible assistant and long-time friend.

Thank you to Doug Webster for your outstanding job as executive director of the National Institute of Youth Ministry (NIYM).

Thank you to the NIYM staff in San Clemente: Tanya Lloyd, Teresa Parsons, Rik Mumma, Ron Spence, Luchi Bierbower, Dean Bruns, Laurie Pilz, Ken Bayard, Russ Cline and Larry Acosta.

Thank you to our 150-plus associate trainers who have been my coworkers, friends and sacrificial guinea pigs.

Thank you to Kyle Duncan, Bill Greig III and Jean Daly for convincing me that Gospel Light is a great publisher who deeply believes in the mission to reach kids. I believe!

Thank you to the Youth Specialties world. Tic, Mike and Wayne, so many years ago, you brought on a wet-behind-the-ears youth worker and taught me most everything I know about youth work today.

Thank you to the hundreds of donors, supporters and friends of NIYM. You are helping create an international grass-roots movement that is helping young people make positive decisions that will affect them for the rest of their lives.

"When there is no counsel, the people fall; But in the multitude of counselors there is safety"
(Proverbs 11:14, *NKJV*)

Jim Burns
San Clemente, CA

# YouthBuilders Group Bible Studies

**It's Relational**—Students learn best when they talk not when you talk. There is always a get acquainted section in the Warm Up. All the experiences are based on building community in your group.

**It's Biblical**—With no apologies, this series in unashamedly Christian. Every session has a practical, relevant Bible study.

**It's Experiential**—Studies show that young people retain up to 85 percent of the material when they are *involved* in action-oriented, experiential learning. The sessions use role plays, discussion starters, case studies, graphs and other experiential, educational methods. *We believe it's a sin to bore a teen with the gospel.*

**It's Interactive**—This study is geared to get students feeling comfortable with sharing ideas and interacting with peers and leaders.

**It's Easy to Follow**—The sessions have been prepared by Jim Burns to allow the leader to pick up the material and use it. There is little preparation time on your part. Jim did the work for you.

**It's Adaptable**—You can pick and choose from several topics or go straight through the material as a whole study.

**It's Parent-oriented**—The Parent Page helps you to do youth ministry at it's finest. Christian education should take place in the home as well as in the church. The Parent Page is your chance to come alongside the parents and help them have a good discussion with their kids.

**It's Proven**—This material was not written by someone in an ivory tower. It was written for, and has already been used with, teens. They love it.

# How to Use This Study

The 12 sessions are divided into three stand-alone units. Each unit has four sessions. You may choose to teach all 12 sessions consecutively. Or you may use only one unit. Or you may present individual sessions. You know your group best so you choose.

Each of the 12 sessions is divided into five sections.

**Warm Up**—This section is designed for you and the students to get to know each other better. These activities are filled with history-giving and affirming questions and experiences.

**Team Effort**—Following the model of Jesus, the Master Teacher, these activities engage teens in the session. Stories, group situations, surveys and more bring the session to the students. There is an option for jr. high/middle school students and one for high school students.

**In the Word**—Most young people are biblically illiterate. These Bible studies present the Word of God and encourage teens to see the relevance of the Scriptures to their lives.

**Things to Think About**—Young people need the opportunity to really think through the issues at hand. These discussion starters get students talking about the subject and interacting on important issues.

**Parent Page**—A youth worker can only do so much. This page allows quality parent/teen communication that really brings the session home.

# THE BIBLE TUCK-IN™

It's a tear-out sheet you fold and place in your Bible, containing the essentials you'll need for teaching your group.

## HERE'S HOW TO USE IT:

To prepare for the session, first study the session. Tear out the Bible *Tuck-In*™ and personalize it by making notes. Fold the Bible *Tuck-In*™ in half on the dotted line. Slip it into your Bible for easy reference throughout the session. The Key Verse, Biblical Basis and Big Idea at the beginning of the Bible *Tuck-In*™ will help you keep the session on track. The information under each section in boldface type is the same as the information on the corresponding student reproducible worksheet. With the Bible *Tuck-In*™ your students will see that your teaching comes from the Bible and won't be distracted by a leader's guide.

## Unit I

# SEX

## LEADER'S PEP TALK

A study recently came across my desk that showed the average 16-year-old male has a sexual thought every 20 seconds! I said that to a crowd of high school students and, of course, got the usual laughs. A young man came up to me after my presentation and said, "Jim, you know that quote about every 20 seconds a 16-year-old male has a sexual thought?" I looked at him, smiled and said, "Yes." He then asked, "So what am I supposed to think about the other 19 seconds? It's always on my mind!" Let's face it, whether we like it or not, young people today are being bombarded with sex and sexual innuendoes. In 1993 the average teenager was able to watch over 14,000 acts of sexual intercourse or innuendo to intercourse on prime-time TV. Advertisers use sexually explicit material to sell anything from blue jeans to cologne. Even cars are sold on TV with a sensual-looking woman displaying a perfect body telling us to go buy her brand of car.

Today's Christian young person will have to go against the grain of the popular culture to choose a Christ-centered lifestyle of sexuality. It isn't easy for them, and it isn't easy for you to teach the "minority view" of sexuality in our culture. However, God created sex (see Genesis 1, 2). In fact, when He created male and female and all the aspects of personhood, including sexuality, He said, "It is very good." Although the Bible is definitely not a sex manual, it does share some very important principles about sex and our actions. This unit is based on the fact that God created sex and, because He loves us, He wants the best for us. That is why He gives us certain guidelines. God is not the Great Killjoy. He wants us to be all that He created us to be.

In this section, you have the opportunity to present biblical sexuality to your students from a positive viewpoint while helping them to "learn to discern" the negative consequences of our actions if we follow the world's standards rather than God's standards.

## BUT WHY DO THEY DO IT?

Authorities tell us that teens are making sexual decisions based on these three reasons:

1. Peer pressure (or the pressure to conform)
   You are in the minority if you haven't had sex by age 18.
2. Emotional involvement that exceeds their maturity level
   Show me a young person with a low self-image who is totally "in love" and I will show you a young person who will be easily seduced sexually.

3. Lack of value-centered education
   Studies are telling us that the more students receive moral and value-centered sex education, the less promiscuous they will be.

As you teach this study, you will help young people make important positive decisions about sex before they get into a tempting situation. You will help them work through the incredible amount of mixed messages they are receiving from school, movies, church, home and friends. You will remind them that God created sex, and it's to be approached with Christ-centered principles and values. You will enable young people to make some very important decisions.

As you look at The Big Idea and Aims of all four sessions, you will see that we are trying to move teens from accepting the standards of the world to developing a lifestyle of biblical standards and morals when it comes to sexuality and relationships. In each of the four sessions you'll have the opportunity to provide information and discussion on a level young people seldom receive. As you deal with these issues remember this verse: "It is God's will that you should be sanctified: that you should avoid sexual immorality" (1 Thessalonians 4:3).

If you can get even one student to follow this advice, it's all worth it.

One last thought, thank you for having the courage to bring up this important issue from a Christian point of view with your young people. As you know, often young people have a difficult time distinguishing between their spirituality and their sexuality and in the next few weeks you will be helping them in both areas of their lives.

# IS GOD THE GREAT KILLJOY?

## **K**EY VERSE

"**T**hen God said, 'Let us make man in our image, in our likeness, and let them rule over the fish of the sea and the birds of the air, over the livestock, over all the earth, and over all the creatures that move along the ground.' God saw all that he had made, and it was very good. And there was evening, and there was morning—the sixth day."
Genesis 1:26,31

## **B**IBLICAL BASIS

**G**enesis 1:26,31; 2:18-25
**E**xodus 20:14
**M**atthew 19:4-6
**G**alatians 5:19,20
**P**hilippians 2:3,4
**H**ebrews 13:4

##  **T**HE BIG IDEA

**G**od created sex, and wants the best for us.

## **A**IMS OF THIS SESSION

**D**uring this session you will guide students to:
• Examine what the Bible says about sexuality;
• Discover that God cares deeply for them and discover His gift of sexuality;
• Thank God for His gift of sex and pray for a biblical understanding of sexuality.

## **W**ARM UP

**The Adam and Eve Quiz**— A quick look at Adam and Eve.

## **T**EAM EFFORT— JUNIOR HIGH/ MIDDLE SCHOOL

**The Island Affair**—A story that forces teens to examine the morality of behavior.

## **T**EAM EFFORT— HIGH SCHOOL

**The Word on Sex**—True and false statements to discover what young people know about God's view of sexuality.

## **I**N THE WORD

**God's True View**—A Bible study on God's view of sexuality and a definition of biblical terms.

## **T**HINGS TO THINK ABOUT (OPTIONAL)

**Q**uestions to get teens thinking and talking about their sexuality.

## **P**ARENT PAGE

**A** tool to get the session into the home and allow parents and teens to discuss Christian principles of sex.

## LEADER'S DEVOTIONAL

Pretend for a moment that ice cream is your favorite thing in life. You'd almost rather eat ice cream than do anything else. You have become, so to speak, sensitized to ice cream-related issues. As you watch TV, an incredible array of ice cream sundaes are shown at their richest and most tantalizing. As you drive down the street, shop after shop where you can indulge your passion for ice cream grabs your attention. Billboards show ice cream, waiting for you in melting, sweet richness. It almost seems that the whole world is somehow ice cream-related!

If you were indeed the person described in the paragraph above, you'd probably eventually come to the conclusion that you were controlled by a passion for ice cream. And the thing you are controlled by, you are also a slave to, the apostle Paul says.

Now think for a minute about what real life was like for you as a teenager. A physically healthy teenager is sex-sensitized. Pause for a moment to remember just how deeply influenced you were by all those hormones that God allowed to pump through your veins!

So, remember: before you will sit a group of sensitized young people who need to know more than what *not* to do. They need to understand what God is up to. After all, how could God make them so ready to have sex and yet tell them not to have it? It seems a cruel joke at first. But let's go back to ice cream. It's not ice cream itself that's a problem. Thousands of people never eat ice cream at all. Ice cream can damage you, addict you, even kill you if it's consumed improperly. But in its place, after a nourishing meal, it's good stuff. In fact, it's great!

Help your students understand that who they are on the *inside* is so important to God that He doesn't want them to misuse anything He's given them. Help them see that sex is good stuff. In fact, it's great! But only in its proper place can it work without damaging and destroying that inner person God loves so much. Sort of the ice cream that rounds out the meal of a good marriage! (Mary Gross, editor, Gospel Light.)

**"God's plan for our pleasure has never changed,... we can be sure that He intended for us to experience full satisfaction in the marriage relationship."—**

Ed Wheat,
*Intended for Pleasure*
(Revell, 1977)

SESSION ONE    BIBLE *TUCK-IN*™

# Is God the Great Killjoy?

## K EY VERSE

"Then God said, 'Let us make man in our image, in our likeness, and let them rule over the fish of the sea and the birds of the air, over the livestock, over all the earth, and over all the creatures that move along the ground.' God saw all that he had made, and it was very good. And there was evening, and there was morning—the sixth day." Genesis 1:26,31

## B IBLICAL BASIS

Genesis 1:26,31; 2:18-25; Exodus 20:14; Matthew 19:4-6; Galatians 5:19,20; Philippians 2:3,4; Hebrews 13:4

## T HE BIG IDEA

God created sex, and wants the best for His children.

## W ARM UP (5-10 MINUTES)

### The Adam and Eve Quiz

• Divide students into two groups.

• Groups compete against each other by calling out the answers to the following questions:

1. Why did Adam have a sore rib cage?
   (God took one of Adam's ribs and made Eve from it.)

2. What were Adam and Eve wearing when they first met?
   (Nothing. They were naked.)

3. What kind of fruit did Eve eat?
   (The Bible doesn't say.)

4. What was the first piece of clothing they wore?
   (God made them garments of animal skin.)

## I N THE WORD (25-30 MINUTES)

### GOD'S TRUE VIEW

• Give each student a copy of "God's True View" on page 25 and a pen or pencil, or display the page using an overhead projector.

• As a whole group complete the Bible study.
**Knowing and understanding what God says about sexuality leads to wholeness in our sexuality.**
**Read Genesis 1:26,31; 2:18-25.**

1. **How do these Scriptures describe humankind? Read Genesis 1:26,31.**
   (Humankind is the greatest of God's creation. Humankind is very good.)

2. **What is God's plan for humankind? Read Genesis 2:18.**
   (God has planned for no substitute or better plan than man and woman in relationship with each other.)

3. **God's ideal is found in the Garden of Eden before the Fall. What is God's ideal for the sexual relationship between a husband and wife? Read Genesis 2:24,25.**
   (Man and woman are to leave all others, be totally committed to each other and be joined in sexual union.)

4. **Consequences follow all our actions. What are the positive consequences for the following:**
   One flesh—two people become one. Sexual intercourse is the most graphic illustration of two people (bodies, spirits and emotions) literally joined as one being. **Read Matthew 19:4-6.**
   (A bond occurs that unites two individuals into one being. This solidifies the commitment of the marriage relationship.)

5. **What are the negative consequences for the following:**
   Adultery—voluntary sexual intercourse between a married person and a person who is not his or her spouse. **Read Exodus 20:14.**
   (The marriage commitment has been violated. Possessiveness, depression, loss of trust, sexually transmitted diseases and unwanted pregnancy may result.)
   **Sexual Immorality or Fornication**—sexual intercourse between two unmarried people. The Greek word *porneia* is usually translated "immorality" but biblical scholars agree that it can also be translated "fornication." (The New Testament was written in Greek.) **Read Galatians 5:19,20.**
   (The physical relationship has exceeded the commitment of the relationship. Possessiveness, depression, feelings of guilt, sexually transmitted diseases and unwanted pregnancy may result.)

## S O WHAT?

**In one sentence, sum up God's view of you and sexuality. Thank God for His gift of sex and pray you will view sexuality as God does.**

## T HINGS TO THINK ABOUT (OPTIONAL)

• Use the questions on page 27 after or as a part of "In the Word."

1. If God created sex and He sees it as very good, why would He ask us to wait until marriage to have sex?

2. Why do you think some people look down on sexuality? Why do you think some people overemphasize sexuality?

3. Read Hebrews 13:4. Why do you think God is so intense about this subject?

## P ARENT PAGE

• Distribute page to parents.

# TEAM EFFORT—JUNIOR HIGH/MIDDLE SCHOOL (15-20 MINUTES)

## THE ISLAND AFFAIR

• Give each student a copy of "The Island Affair" on page 21 and a pen or pencil, or display the page using an overhead projector.

• Students individually read the story and rate the characters.

• As a whole group, students discuss the ratings they gave each person in the story and then answer the last question on the page.

**1. Rate each person from 1 (the best person) to 5 (the worst person).**

...... Albert

...... Bruno

...... Carla

...... Della

...... Edgar

**2. What do you think each person thinks about sex?**

Albert

Bruno

Carla

Della

Edgar

- - - - - - - - - - - - - - - - - Fold - - - - - - - - - - - - - - - -

# TEAM EFFORT—HIGH SCHOOL (15-20 MINUTES)

## THE WORD ON SEX

• Give each student a copy of "The Word on Sex" on page 23 and a pen or pencil.

• Students individually answer statements and give a reason for their answers.

• As a whole group, students report answers and reasons for answers. For each statement, circle T for true or F for false. Then give a reason for your answer.

**1. T or F**     The Bible is old-fashioned and out of date on the subject of sexuality.

**2. T or F**     Sexual intercourse before marriage is a sin.

**3. T or F**     The Bible says sex is good.

**4. T or F**     Christians should avoid sex.

**5. T or F**     Most teens don't have a good understanding of sex and sexuality.

**6. T or F**     The majority of teens will have sexual intercourse before they become adults.

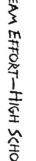

# TEAM EFFORT

## THE ISLAND AFFAIR[1]

The two circles represent two islands surrounded by shark-infested waters. As a result of a shipwreck, only five survivors manage to reach the safety of the islands. Albert is separated from his fiancee, Carla. Carla is stranded on the other island with her mother, Della. Bruno, a young man of about the same age as Albert, ends up on Albert's island. The fifth survivor is an older man, Edgar. He is a loner and on the same island with Carla and Della.

Albert and Carla are deeply in love. After two months of being separated yet seeing each other across the water, they desperately long to be together, but each passing day makes rescue look more hopeless. Carla becomes despondent. One day while walking around the island, Carla discovers a crude boat hollowed out of an old tree. It looks seaworthy. Then Edgar appears. He has just finished making the boat. Carla explains her longing to reach the other island to be with Albert and pleads with Edgar to let her have the boat. Edgar refuses, saying the boat was made for his escape and not hers. After Carla's incessant pleading, Edgar proposes that if Carla will make love to him, he will take her to the other island in his boat. Carla asks for time to consider and runs to find Della. She explains to her mother that rescue looks hopeless and that if they are to be stranded on an island, she should at least be with the one she loves. Della listens with understanding and after much thought says, "I know you sincerely love Albert and I understand your desire to be with him, but I am afraid the cost is a bit high. It is up to you to do what you want, but my advice would be to wait a bit longer. I'm sure a better solution will come, and you will be glad you waited." Carla considers her mother's advice for a number of days. Finally, she decides to accept Edgar's offer. Carla makes love to Edgar. Edgar keeps his part of the bargain and rows Carla to Albert's island. Albert and Carla embrace and are very happy, but during the day's conversation, Carla confesses that she made love to Edgar only because she loved Albert so much. Albert is deeply hurt. He tells Carla that although he loves her very much, he cannot continue their relationship knowing that she has made love to another man. Carla tries to change Albert's mind but to no avail.

During their discussion, Bruno is listening from behind some bushes. When Albert leaves, Bruno comes to Carla and explains that he thinks what she did was admirable. He understands that her experience with Edgar was the result of desperation and was an act of love for Albert. Bruno tells Carla that he would readily accept someone who would pay such a high price for their love and he would be willing to care for Carla in spite of what Albert did. Carla accepts.

**1. Rate each person from 1 (the best person) to 5 (the worst person).**

...... **Albert**

...... **Bruno**

...... **Carla**

...... **Della**

...... **Edgar**

**2. What do you think each person thinks about sex?**

**Albert** ..........................................................................................

**Bruno** ..........................................................................................

**Carla** ..........................................................................................

**Della** ..........................................................................................

**Edgar** ..........................................................................................

**Note**

1. Jim Burns and Mike Yaconelli, *High School Ministry* (Grand Rapids, MI: Zondervan, 1986), p. 252 ff. Used by permission.

## TEAM EFFORT

### THE WORD ON SEX

For each statement, circle *T* for true or *F* for false. Then give a reason for your answer.

**1. T or F**    The Bible is old-fashioned and out of date on the subject of sexuality.

.......................................................................................................................................

.......................................................................................................................................

**2. T or F**    Sexual intercourse before marriage is a sin.

.......................................................................................................................................

.......................................................................................................................................

**3. T or F**    The Bible says sex is very good.

.......................................................................................................................................

.......................................................................................................................................

**4. T or F**    Christians should avoid sex.

.......................................................................................................................................

.......................................................................................................................................

**5. T or F**    Most teens don't have a good understanding of sex and sexuality.

.......................................................................................................................................

.......................................................................................................................................

**6. T or F**    The majority of teens will have sexual intercourse before they become adults.

.......................................................................................................................................

.......................................................................................................................................

# IN THE WORD

## GOD'S TRUE VIEW

Knowing and understanding what God says about sexuality leads to wholeness in our sexuality.
Read Genesis 1:26,31; 2:18-25.

**1.** How do these Scriptures describe humankind? Read Genesis 1:26,31.

.................................................................................

.................................................................................

**2.** What is God's plan for humankind? Read Genesis 2:18.

.................................................................................

.................................................................................

**3.** God's ideal is found in the Garden of Eden before the Fall. What is God's ideal for the sexual relationship between a husband and wife? Read Genesis 2:24,25.

.................................................................................

.................................................................................

**4.** Consequences follow all our actions. What are the positive consequences of the following:

| ACTION | CONSEQUENCES |
|---|---|
| One flesh—two people become one. Sexual intercourse is the most graphic illustration of two people (bodies, spirits and emotions) literally joined as one. Read Matthew 19:4-6. | .................... .................... .................... .................... .................... |

**5.** What are the negative consequences of the following:

| ACTION | CONSEQUENCES |
|---|---|
| Adultery—voluntary sexual intercourse between a married person and a partner who is not his or her spouse. Read Exodus 20:14. | .................... .................... .................... |
| Sexual Immorality or Fornication—sexual intercourse between unmarried partners. The Greek word *porneia* is usually translated "immorality" but biblical scholars agree that it also can be translated "fornication." (The New Testament was written in Greek.) Read Galatians 5:19,20. | .................... .................... .................... .................... .................... .................... .................... |

# SO WHAT?

In one sentence, sum up God's view of
you and sexuality. Thank God for His
gift of sex and pray that you will view
sexuality as God does........................

.................................................................................

.................................................................................

.................................................................................

.................................................................................

.................................................................................

# THINGS TO THINK ABOUT

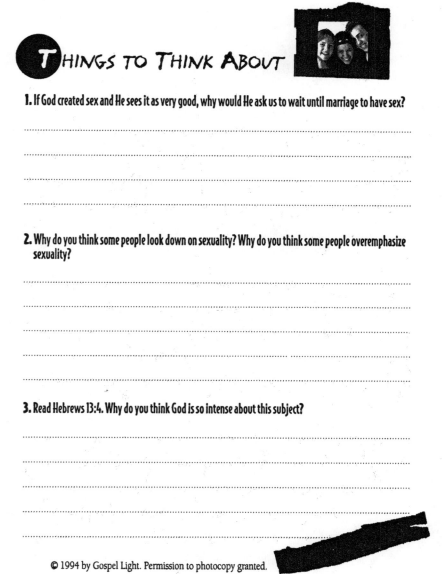

**1.** If God created sex and He sees it as very good, why would He ask us to wait until marriage to have sex?

.........................................................................................

.........................................................................................

.........................................................................................

.........................................................................................

**2.** Why do you think some people look down on sexuality? Why do you think some people overemphasize sexuality?

.........................................................................................

.........................................................................................

.........................................................................................

.........................................................................................

.........................................................................................

**3.** Read Hebrews 13:4. Why do you think God is so intense about this subject?

.........................................................................................

.........................................................................................

.........................................................................................

.........................................................................................

.........................................................................................

# PARENT PAGE

"Do nothing out of selfish ambition or vain conceit, but in humility consider others better than yourselves. Each of you should look not only to your own interests, but to the interests of others" (Philippians 2:3,4).

### 1. What is the main idea of this Scripture?

.......................................................................................................

.......................................................................................................

.......................................................................................................

.......................................................................................................

.......................................................................................................

### 2. How does that idea relate to our sexuality?

.......................................................................................................

.......................................................................................................

.......................................................................................................

.......................................................................................................

## ADVICE FOR TERRI

Terri is a student leader in the church youth group. As a student leader she has made a commitment not to have sex until marriage. *However*, she has fallen in love with Ron. They both know that the way things are going they will soon be sleeping together. Terri does love Ron and believes one day they will get married. She wants to live her life by Christian principles. She has come to you for help and advice. Decide together what you will say to Terri.

**Session 1 "Is God the Great Killjoy?" Date**................................

# INFLUENCES

## KEY VERSE

"It is God's will that you should be sanctified; that you should avoid sexual immorality."
1 Thessalonians 4:3

## BIBLICAL BASIS

Matthew 5:27-30;
Ephesians 5:3-5;
1 Thessalonians 4:1-8

## THE BIG IDEA

The Bible's view of sexuality and the media's view of sexuality differ. Young people need to discern between the two views.

## AIMS OF THIS SESSION

During this session you will guide students to:
• Examine the media's influence on sexuality;
• Discover how the Bible's true view of sexuality differs from the media's view;
• Identify one way the media has negatively influenced them and make appropriate changes.

## WARM UP

"It's in Our Music" Contest—
A contest to realize how many songs address sex.

## Team Effort— Junior High/ Middle School

Sex Sells—A search for sex in advertisements.

## TEAM EFFORT— HIGH SCHOOL

Who's Really Influencing Teens About Sex?—
A rating of what influences teens' view of sexuality.

## IN THE WORD

God's Standards vs. the Movies—A Bible study on sexual standards and a comparison with the movies' portrayal of sexuality.

## THINGS TO THINK ABOUT (OPTIONAL)

Questions to get teens thinking and talking about culture's emphasis on sex.

## PARENT PAGE

A tool to get the session into the home and allow parents and teens to discuss who and what influences our views of sexuality.

## Leader's Devotional

Society has sent all of us powerful messages about sex and about relationship. We've been sent (through many generations of books, stories, songs, plays and movies) one very subtle, yet extremely damaging message: that sex can be divorced from relationship and still satisfy. Sex is often portrayed as a one-dimensional act of physical performance, making relationship not only unnecessary, but even undesirable. The irony is that the opposite message is often sent at the same time: that this sexual performance somehow will *create* relationship between two people. Is it any wonder we've all been a bit confused at some point?

The damage and confusion contrast powerfully with God's high view of relationship. He has focused all His love and grace on establishing valuable relationship between Himself and us! He has given us the power as His children to foster and to value healthy relationships among ourselves. Relationship is number one with Him!

But before teaching, check the personal relationship index. Consider what other conflicting messages may be sent—by us, adult leaders. Remember that even with young people this age, more is still "caught than taught." As we teach, our body language, tone of voice and the attitudes we display will tell more than what we say! What are your true feelings about these students to whom you relate? What is *your* honest attitude toward sex? Your genuine feelings about male-female relationships? Your true attitude toward the media? The attitudes we show need to exemplify what we say about the value of relationship and about the value God places on each of us! Ask God to shape your nonverbal teaching as well as your words into the unmixed message of loving relationship that He wants your teens to see—and from which they'll learn.
(Mary Gross, editor, Gospel Light.)

"The media doesn't make it seem like it's really all about love. Nowadays sexuality is the way you look....It's all physical, not what's inside you."—

Seventeen-year-old girl,
*Time*, May 24, 1993

# SESSION TWO    BIBLE TUCK-IN™

# INFLUENCES

## Key Verse

"It is God's will that you should be sanctified; that you should avoid sexual immorality." 1 Thessalonians 4:3

## Biblical Basis

Matthew 5:27-30; Ephesians 5:3-5; 1 Thessalonians 4:1-8

## The Big Idea

The Bible's view of sexuality and the media's view of sexuality differ. Young people need to discern between the two views.

## Warm Up (5-10 Minutes)

"It's in Our Music" Contest

• Divide students into groups of three or four.
• Provide pencil or pen and paper for someone in each group to write a list.
• Students list as many song titles having to do with sex as they can. Remind them that the goal is to come up with as many as possible, not to come up with the most shocking.
• After approximately two minutes find out which group wrote the most song titles (the world's record is 30!).
• Ask each group to share some of the song titles.

---Fold---

## In the Word (25-30 Minutes)

### God's Standards vs. the Movies

• Divide students into pairs.
• Give each student a copy of "God's Standards vs. the Movies" on page 37 and a pen or pencil.
• Students complete the Bible study.

The year is 2225. You do not have access to a Bible, but you do have three separate Scriptures relating to sex. You have been asked to develop biblical standards in regards to movies. Read the Scriptures and develop at least five standards.
Matthew 5:27-30
Ephesians 5:3-5
1 Thessalonians 4:1-8

1. .......................................................................
2. .......................................................................
3. .......................................................................
4. .......................................................................
5. .......................................................................

(Possible standards: keep our minds pure; avoid anything that causes you to sin in thought or deed; keep away from anything that even looks like sin; all our conversations should be pure; immoral people won't be part of God's kingdom; we should avoid immorality; we control ourselves; we are to live holy lives.)

In light of the standards you've just developed, answer the following questions:

1. What movie presents God's view of sexuality?

2. Is it okay for actors and actresses to act in the nude or in sexually explicit scenes since they are "only acting"? Why or why not?

3. Why do you think movies today contain so much sexually explicit material? What is its purpose?

4. Do you believe that the movies present an accurate portrayal of sexuality or male/female relationships?

5. Do you think Christians should view sexually explicit films? Why or why not? Would the age or maturity of the viewer be a factor in this regard?

## So What?

What negative effect have sexually explicit movies (or magazines or songs, etc.) had on you? On your relationship to others? On your relationship to God? What can you do to avoid this negative influence?

## Things to Think About (optional)

• Use the questions on page 39 after or as a part of "In the Word."
1. Why are we so curious about sex?
2. At times it seems our society is "sex crazy." Who's to blame?
3. Who or what in our culture is portraying a positive biblical view of sexuality?

## Parent Page

• Distribute page to parents.

# TEAM EFFORT—JUNIOR HIGH/MIDDLE SCHOOL (15-20 MINUTES)

## SEX SELLS

• Ask students to name some TV commercials that use sex and sexual innuendos.

• Divide students into groups of three or four.

• Provide a variety of magazines (sports, glamour, news, music, etc. [at least one per person]).

• Students look through the magazines to find the most sexually explicit ads. Show an example to get them thinking in the right direction. For example beer, jeans and perfume commercials almost always use sexual innuendos.

• Then students find the most subtle advertising that uses sex. Again show an example.

• Ask the students to "show and tell" what they find.

---

# TEAM EFFORT—HIGH SCHOOL (15-20 MINUTES)

## WHO'S REALLY INFLUENCING TEENS ABOUT SEX?

• Divide students into groups of three or four.

• Give each student a copy of "Who's Really Influencing Teens About Sex?" on page 35 and a pen or pencil, or display the page using an overhead projector.

• Students rate each influence.

• As a whole group, try to develop a consensus of ratings. Everyone is influenced when it comes to the subject of sexuality. Who and what influences the average teenager the most? Rate the influences from 1 (the most influential) to 13 (the least influential).

| Music | 1. |
| TV | 2. |
| Parent | 3. |
| Brother/Sister | 4. |
| Movies | 5. |
| Government | 6. |
| Youth Worker | 7. |
| Teachers | 8. |
| Friends | 9. |
| Books | 10. |
| Church | 11. |
| Advertisements | 12. |
| Bible | 13. |

Fold

 *T*EAM *E*FFORT

## WHO'S REALLY INFLUENCING TEENS ABOUT SEX?

Everyone is influenced when it comes to the subject of sexuality. Who and what influences the average teenager the most? Rate the influences from 1 (the most influential) to 13 (the least influential).

| | |
|---|---|
| **Music** | 1. ..................................................................................... |
| **TV** | 2. ..................................................................................... |
| **Parent** | 3. ..................................................................................... |
| **Brother/Sister** | 4. ..................................................................................... |
| **Movies** | 5. ..................................................................................... |
| **Government** | 6. ..................................................................................... |
| **Youth Worker** | 7. ..................................................................................... |
| **Teachers** | 8. ..................................................................................... |
| **Friends** | 9. ..................................................................................... |
| **Books** | 10. ..................................................................................... |
| **Church** | 11. ..................................................................................... |
| **Advertisements** | 12. ..................................................................................... |
| **Bible** | 13. ..................................................................................... |

Now that you've put this together, as a group try to come up with a consensus.

# IN THE WORD

## GOD'S STANDARDS VS. THE MOVIES

The year is 2225. You do not have access to a Bible, but you do have three separate Scriptures relating to sex. You have been asked to develop biblical standards in regards to movies. Read the Scriptures and develop at least five standards.

Matthew 5:27-30
Ephesians 5:3-5
1 Thessalonians 4:1-8

1. ........................................................................

2. ........................................................................

3. ........................................................................

4. ........................................................................

5. ........................................................................

In light of the standards you've just developed, answer the following questions:

1. What movie presents God's view of sexuality?

........................................................................

2. Is it okay for actors and actresses to act in the nude or in sexually explicit scenes since they are "only acting"? Why or why not?

........................................................................

3. Why do you think movies today contain so much sexually explicit material? What is its purpose?

........................................................................

4. Do you believe that the movies present an accurate portrayal of sexuality or male/female relationships?

........................................................................

5. Do you think Christians should view sexually explicit films? Why or why not? Would the age or maturity of the viewer be a factor in this regard?

........................................................................

# SO WHAT?

What negative effect have sexually explicit movies (or magazines or songs, etc.) had on you? On your relationship to others? On your relationship to God? What can you do to avoid this negative influence?

........................................................................

........................................................................

........................................................................

........................................................................

........................................................................

#  THINGS TO THINK ABOUT

**1.** Why are we so curious about sex?

.................................................................................................

.................................................................................................

.................................................................................................

.................................................................................................

.................................................................................................

**2.** At times it seems our society is "sex crazy." Who's to blame?

.................................................................................................

.................................................................................................

.................................................................................................

.................................................................................................

.................................................................................................

**3.** Who or what in our culture is portraying a positive biblical view of sexuality?

.................................................................................................

.................................................................................................

.................................................................................................

.................................................................................................

.................................................................................................

# PARENT PAGE

## INTERVIEW QUESTIONS FOR PARENT FROM TEEN

**1.** What was your worst date?

**2.** What was your best date?

**3.** How did you hear about sex?

**4.** What was the best piece of advice you ever received about sex?

**5.** What concerns you most about the media's view of sexuality and its influence?

**Session 2 "Influences" Date**...................................

## INTERVIEW QUESTIONS FOR TEEN FROM PARENT

**1.** What would be your ultimate date?

**2.** Where do you receive the most input about sex?
   a. TV
   b. movies
   c. music
   d. parent
   e. friends
   f. church
   g. other...........

**3.** What annoys you most about sex?

**4.** If you could give a good friend one piece of advice about sex what would it be?

**5.** If you could give Madonna one piece of advice about sex what would it be?

# TAKING THE SEXUAL PURITY CHALLENGE

## **K** EY VERSE

"Flee from sexual immorality. All other sins a man commits are outside his body, but he who sins sexually sins against his own body. Do you not know that your body is a temple of the Holy Spirit, who is in you, whom you have received from God? You are not your own; you were bought at a price. Therefore honor God with your body."
1 Corinthians 6:18-20

## **B** IBLICAL BASIS

**1** Corinthians 6:18-20
**E** phesians 5:3
**1** Thessalonians 4:1-8
**1** Peter 2:11

## **T** HE BIG IDEA

Teens need to commit their bodies to God and refrain from sexual intercourse until marriage.

## **A** IMS OF THIS SESSION

During this session you will guide students to:
• Examine the possibility of living a life of sexual abstinence until marriage;
• Discover the biblical basis for giving their bodies and sexual standards to God;
• Implement a decision to take The Sexual Purity Challenge and honor God with their bodies.

## **W** ARM UP

**Cared for and Loved—**
A survey of young people's preferences and limits.

## **T** EAM EFFORT— JUNIOR HIGH/ MIDDLE SCHOOL

**The Premarital Sex Quiz—**
An agree/disagree activity on the opinions of premarital sex.

## **T** EAM EFFORT— HIGH SCHOOL

**Why Wait?—**
A discussion of important considerations regarding premarital sex.

## **I** N THE WORD

**The Sexual Purity Challenge—**
A Bible study of God's command for sexual purity.

## **T** HINGS TO THINK ABOUT (OPTIONAL)

Questions to get teens thinking and talking about premarital sex.

## **P** ARENT PAGE

A tool to get the session into the home and allow parents and teens to discuss premarital sex.

## LEADER'S DEVOTIONAL

If you've ever been a young person, you've probably experienced the high anxiety that goes along with that big rite of passage, the driver's license. You also know that when you are 15, everyone *except* you has their learner's permit and is on the road day and night with someone who will teach them what they need to know to pass the dreaded test. You are the only one left out! Until you have a driver's license, you're sure you are nothing, a social outcast destined to never go anywhere in life—literally! So you gotta have it, *now*.

If this is so important, why on earth do we heartless adults and the Department of Motor Vehicles operate in denial mode? Why do we require a license before they get behind the wheel? Simply this: We know how easy it is to be damaged or killed by driving a car. So an understanding of the rules of the road, a smattering of practice in a safe environment and proof of commitment (that's insurance) are required before we say, "Okay. You're ready. Here's a license."

Sex isn't much different. To a teen, it seems like he or she is the *only one* in the world who is still a virgin. It seems that the only way to get respect as a full-fledged man or woman is to have sex. And of course, you need to do it *now*.

There's a license for this one, too. Complete relationship is a more dangerous thing than driving, requiring lots of risk taking. And we all know how easily damage can result if a complete relationship (the kind that includes sexual intercourse) isn't handled with the respect it deserves.

True, granting a couple a wedding license doesn't prove that either of them will be an enjoyable mate, a terrific sexual partner or even a person who regularly takes out the garbage. But for a Christian couple prepared by the Spirit of God and wise helpers, it shows they understand the "rules of the road." They've probably gotten in some practice in relating. And most important, they're committed to the idea of staying together exclusively. Commitment is what will make them willing to work on taking out the garbage and being a better mate. It's the license to have before two people get into a bed together. (Mary Gross, editor, Gospel Light.)

**"Sex outside of marital commitment is only full of fear and anxiety. We shouldn't give ourselves fully until we get a commitment."—**

Lisa Peluso, actress, *Mademoiselle*, March 1994

# TAKING THE SEXUAL PURITY CHALLENGE

## Key Verse

"Flee from sexual immorality. All other sins a man commits are outside his body, but he who sins sexually sins against his own body. Do you not know that your body is a temple of the Holy Spirit, who is in you, whom you have received from God? You are not your own; you were bought at a price. Therefore honor God with your body." 1 Corinthians 6:18-20

## Biblical Basis

1 Corinthians 6:18-20; Ephesians 5:3; 1 Thessalonians 4:1-8; 1 Peter 2:11

## The Big Idea

Teens need to commit their bodies to God and refrain from sexual intercourse until marriage.

## Warm Up (5-10 Minutes)

CARED FOR AND LOVED

• Divide students into groups according to their year in school.
• Display a copy of "Cared for and Loved" page 47 using an overhead projector.
• Students answer questions.

1. As a child, what person, place in your home, time of year, etc. made you feel cared for and loved?
2. When did you discover that God cares for and loves you?

---

Fold

---

---

3. Read 1 Corinthians 6:20.

a. Write this verse in your own words.

b. According to this verse, what's our response to Christ's love for us?

c. The Sexual Purity Challenge is to commit our sexuality to God and refrain from sexual intercourse until marriage. Why would this be a proper response to our commitment to God?

## So What?

Are you willing to take The Sexual Purity Challenge today? If so, sign and date the pledge.

### The Sexual Purity Pledge

Believing that God's best for my life and others is to keep my life sexually pure and refrain from sexual intercourse until the day I enter marriage, I commit my body to God, my future mate and my family.

_____     _____
signature                                            date

## Things to Think About (Optional)

• Use the questions on page 55 after or as a part of "In the Word."

1. What keeps people from refraining from sexual intercourse until marriage?

2. Is it realistic in today's culture to really remain a virgin until marriage? Why or why not?

3. What one question about sex would you like to ask God?

## Parent Page

• Distribute page to parents.

# TEAM EFFORT—JUNIOR HIGH/MIDDLE SCHOOL (15-20 MINUTES)

## THE PREMARITAL SEX QUIZ

- Give each student a red slip of paper and a green slip of paper.
- Display a copy of "The Premarital Sex Quiz" on page 47 using an overhead projector.
- Read aloud each statement.
- If students agree with the statement, they hold up green slips of paper. If students disagree, they hold up red slips of paper.
- Discuss each statement.

1. Being in love justifies premarital sex.
2. If you're not ready for marriage, you're not ready for sexual intercourse.
3. Premarital sex bases a relationship on physical aspects.
4. Premarital sex must be wrong because couples have to sneak to do it.
5. Premarital sex offers a false sense of intimacy.
6. People who have premarital sex are likely to cheat on their spouses after they are married.
7. Love needs to be expressed through sexual intercourse.
8. Premarital sex provides people with a needed sexual release.
9. Premarital sex makes a person feel wanted, cared about and appreciated.
10. Having premarital sex will affect your reputation.

# TEAM EFFORT—HIGH SCHOOL (15-20 MINUTES)

## WHY WAIT?

- Display a copy of "Why Wait?" on page 49 using an overhead projector.
- As a whole group, discuss each question.

Here are 11 questions to consider regarding premarital sex:

1. Will premarital sex lessen the meaning of sex in marriage for either of you?
2. Does (or would) your conscience make you feel uneasy during or after sexual intercourse?
3. Are you both equally committed to each other?
4. Are you totally convinced in your hearts that the other person is "the one" forever?
5. What do you believe the Bible has to say about premarital sex? Now read Ephesians 5:3; 1 Thessalonians 4:1-8; 1 Peter 2:11.
6. Will having sexual intercourse affect your usefulness to God or your relationship with Him?

7. Will having sex before marriage damage, in any way, your relationship with each other?
8. Could premarital sex damage your communication? Could it cause you to lose respect for your special friend? Could it cause you to mistrust him or her?
9. Will premarital sex help, hinder or not affect your spiritual relationship to each other?
10. Have you thought through the possibilities of parenthood, marriage because of a pregnancy, and birth control?
11. What are your motives for having premarital sex? Are they pure?

# IN THE WORD (20-25 MINUTES)

## THE SEXUAL PURITY CHALLENGE

- Divide students into groups of three or four. Make sure each group has at least one guy and one girl.
- Display a copy of "The Sexual Purity Challenge" on pages 51 and 53 using an overhead projector.
- Students complete the Bible study.
The Sexual Purity Challenge is to commit our sexuality to God and refrain from sexual intercourse until marriage.

1. Read 1 Corinthians 6:18.
a. Write this verse in your own words.
b. Why does the Bible say to flee from sexual immorality?
c. How is sexual sin different from other sins? Even though all sin is literally "missing the mark" and "falling short of God's glory," according to this Scripture a sexual sin tends to stay with us longer because it's a sin against our own body.

2. Read 1 Corinthians 6:19.
a. Write this verse in your own words.
b. How does this verse relate to your relationship with the opposite sex?
c. Christians are called to respect one another. What does that mean according to this verse? Christians are to approach dating and relating to the opposite sex differently than the world's standards. They are called to "radically respect." Why? Because you have the Holy Spirit of God dwelling inside of you. Imagine this conversation:

Glen, you are not just dating Jill, who is beautiful, with a wonderful smile and a great personality, you are dating Jill who has the very Spirit of God dwelling inside of her. Honor her as you would any sister in Christ. Jill, you aren't just dating Glen, this hunk of a guy with such good looks and a great personality, you are also dating Glen who has the Holy Spirit of God living inside of him. The Bible says "...out do one another in showing honor" (Romans 12:10, BSV). You are called to radically respect each other.

# WARM UP

## CARED FOR AND LOVED

**1.** As a child, what person, place in your home, time of year, etc. made you feel cared for and loved?

..................................................................................................................

..................................................................................................................

..................................................................................................................

**2.** When did you discover that God cares for and loves you?

..................................................................................................................

..................................................................................................................

..................................................................................................................

# TEAM EFFORT

## THE PREMARITAL SEX QUIZ[1]

1. Being in love justifies premarital sex.
2. If you're not ready for marriage, you're not ready for sexual intercourse.
3. Premarital sex bases a relationship on physical aspects.
4. Premarital sex must be wrong because couples have to sneak to do it.
5. Premarital sex offers a false sense of intimacy.
6. People who have premarital sex are likely to cheat on their spouses after they are married.
7. Love needs to be expressed through sexual intercourse.
8. Premarital sex provides people with a needed sexual release.
9. Premarital sex makes a person feel wanted, cared about and appreciated.
10. Having premarital sex will affect your reputation.

**Note**
1. David Lynn and Mike Yaconelli, *Teaching the Truth About Sex* (Grand Rapids, MI: Zondervan, Youth Specialties, 1990), p. 100. Used by permission.

# TEAM EFFORT

## WHY WAIT?

Here are 11 questions to consider regarding premarital sex:

**1.** Will premarital sex lessen the meaning of sex in marriage for either of you?

.................................................................................................

**2.** Does (or would) your conscience make you feel uneasy during or after sexual intercourse?

.................................................................................................

**3.** Are you both equally committed to each other?

.................................................................................................

**4.** Are you totally convinced in your hearts that the other person is "the one" forever?

.................................................................................................

**5.** What do you believe the Bible has to say about premarital sex? Now read Ephesians 5:3; 1 Thessalonians 4:1-8; 1 Peter 2:11.

.................................................................................................

**6.** Will having sexual intercourse affect your usefulness to God or your relationship with Him?

.................................................................................................

**7.** Will having sex before marriage damage, in any way, your relationship with each other?

.................................................................................................

**8.** Could premarital sex damage your communication? Could it cause you to lose respect for your special friend? Could it cause you to mistrust him or her?

.................................................................................................

**9.** Will premarital sex help, hinder or not affect your spiritual relationship to each other?

.................................................................................................

**10.** Have you thought through the possibilities of parenthood, marriage because of a pregnancy, and birth control?

.................................................................................................

**11.** What are your motives for having premarital sex? Are they pure?

.................................................................................................

# 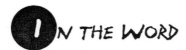 IN THE WORD

## THE SEXUAL PURITY CHALLENGE

The Sexual Purity Challenge is to commit our sexuality to God and refrain from sexual intercourse until marriage.

**1. Read 1 Corinthians 6:18.**

**a. Write this verse in your own words.**

......................................................................................................

......................................................................................................

**b. Why does the Bible say to flee from sexual immorality?**

......................................................................................................

......................................................................................................

**c. How is sexual sin different from other sins?**

......................................................................................................

......................................................................................................

Even though all sin is literally "missing the mark" and "falling short of God's glory," according to this Scripture a sexual sin tends to stay with us longer because it's a sin against our own body.

**2. Read 1 Corinthians 6:19.**

**a. Write this verse in your own words.**

......................................................................................................

......................................................................................................

**b. How does this verse relate to your relationship with the opposite sex?**

......................................................................................................

......................................................................................................

**c. Christians are called to respect one another. What does that mean according to this verse?**

......................................................................................................

......................................................................................................

**CHRISTIANS ARE TO APPROACH** dating and relating to the opposite sex differently than the world's standards. They are called to "radically respect." Why? Because you have the Holy Spirit of God dwelling inside of you. Imagine this conversation:

**GLEN, YOU ARE NOT JUST** dating Jill, who is beautiful, with a wonderful smile and a great personality, you are dating Jill who has the very Spirit of God dwelling inside of her. Honor her as you would any sister in Christ. Jill, you aren't just dating Glen, this hunk of a guy with such good looks and a great personality, you are also dating Glen who has the Holy Spirit of God living inside of him. The Bible says "out do one another in showing honor" (Romans 12:10, RSV). You are called to radically respect each other.

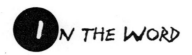 **IN THE WORD**

3. Read 1 Corinthians 6:20.
   a. Write this verse in your own words.

........................................................................................................

........................................................................................................

........................................................................................................

   b. According to this verse, what's our response to Christ's love for us?

........................................................................................................

........................................................................................................

........................................................................................................

   c. The Sexual Purity Challenge is to commit our sexuality to God and refrain from sexual intercourse until marriage. Why would this be a proper response to our commitment to God?

........................................................................................................

........................................................................................................

........................................................................................................

**SO WHAT?**

Are you willing to take The Sexual Purity Challenge today? If so, sign and date the pledge.

## THE SEXUAL PURITY PLEDGE

Believing that God's best for my life and others is to keep my life sexually pure and refrain from sexual intercourse until the day I enter marriage, I commit my body to God, my future mate and my family.

........................................................................................................
signature                                    date

# Things to Think About

**1.** What keeps people from refraining from sexual intercourse until marriage?

.......................................................................................

.......................................................................................

.......................................................................................

.......................................................................................

**2.** Is it realistic in today's culture to really remain a virgin until marriage? Why or why not?

.......................................................................................

.......................................................................................

.......................................................................................

.......................................................................................

**3.** What one question about sex would you like to ask God?

.......................................................................................

.......................................................................................

.......................................................................................

# PARENT PAGE

In the book *Radical Respect: A Christian Approach to Love, Sex and Dating*, there is a chapter on The Sexual Purity Challenge. Letters are received every day from ordinary people who are making an extraordinary decision for God and for themselves. Thousands of young people have taken The Sexual Purity Challenge.
Together read this letter.

## DEAR JIM,

My name is Lori and I am 13 years old going on 14. I'm reading your book *Radical Respect*. I have a story I have needed to share with someone for a very long time and I am asking you to please listen to my story.

Five months ago I lost my virginity to a man who meant nothing to me. He was a friend of my "best friend." The day I met him we hit it right off. The next evening we started going out. Eventually we began to make out. Soon he began to say he loved me. Well I thought I loved him, too.

One day my friend (who's not a virgin either) suggested sex. Well I "loved" him so why not? I knew I wasn't ready, but my girlfriend ended up talking me into it. Two weeks after we began going out we were in bed together. Back then I was not close to God so premarital sex meant nothing to me. Two months later I began to show. I was pregnant. Finally I got up the courage to tell my boyfriend. That night he dumped me. I cried so much after that. I was torn apart. I even tried to commit suicide. First I tried to slit my wrists, but the sight of my own blood made me chicken out. Then I tried overdosing myself with 500 mg. extra-strength Tylenol and Excedrin. I ended up with a bad stomachache and nothing more. It was a miracle, God obviously wanted me alive.

To make a long story short, I had a miscarriage! After my boyfriend found out he asked me back but I said no.

I'm glad I've finally had the chance to get that out. I feel so relieved. Lately, I have been doing much better and feel myself growing closer to Christ. I have already asked for forgiveness and taken The Sexual Purity Challenge. I have also asked Jesus into my life and heart. I pray all the time and have quit some of my very sinful habits thanks to your book. It has really helped me find my faith. Well thank you for your time.
Love,

LORI

## Now discuss these issues:

• Consequences
• Family communication
• Positive Decisions
• Forgiveness

Session 3 "Taking the Sexual Purity Challenge" Date.............................

# HOW FAR IS TOO FAR?

## **K**EY VERSE

"**N**o temptation has seized you except what is common to man. And God is faithful; he will not let you be tempted beyond what you can bear. But when you are tempted, he will also provide a way out so that you can stand up under it."
1 Corinthians 10:13

## **B**IBLICAL BASIS

**1** Corinthians 10:13; 13:4-7

## **T**HE BIG IDEA

**Y**oung people need to set standards before they are in a tempting situation. The decisions they make today will affect them for a lifetime.

## **A**IMS OF THIS SESSION

**D**uring this session you will guide students to:
- Examine the often asked question: How far is too far?;
- Discover God's principles for setting sexual standards;
- Set biblical sexual standards.

## **W**ARM UP

**TAKE IT TO THE LIMIT**—
A survey of teens' preferences and limits.

## **T**EAM EFFORT— JUNIOR HIGH/ MIDDLE SCHOOL

**THE RELATIONSHIP GRAPH**—
An evaluation of two relationships.

## **T**EAM EFFORT— HIGH SCHOOL

**HOW FAR SHOULD I GO?**—
A chart of appropriate sexual behavior at each stage of a relationship.

## **I**N THE WORD

**SHOWING TRUE LOVE**—
A Bible study on showing true love in a dating relationship.

## **T**HINGS TO THINK ABOUT (OPTIONAL)

**Q**uestions to get teens thinking and talking about sexual standards.

## **P**ARENT PAGE

**A** tool to get the session into the home and allow parents and teens to discuss appropriate dating relationships.

## LEADER'S DEVOTIONAL

Because God made us in His image both inside and out, He treats us with the respect due to a work of His creation. He not only sees us warts and all, but He also knows us deep inside. The person we think nobody knows is open before Him! And He values that inner person in each of us far more than even we do.

Satan, on the other hand, loves to foster disrespect. It's a usual vehicle for laughs in situation comedies; it's defended in songs and movies as "standing your ground" and "respecting yourself," a kind of fierce self-protection that means everyone else better give way. And frankly, in our society, we admire this ruggedly individualistic mentality. Disrespect destroys relationship. And we've learned that respect and relationship are what God seeks to build.

On this issue of deciding how far is too far, we can be assured that most every young person has (consciously or unconsciously) already drawn some lines for him- or herself. But these lines may not be ones they will talk about readily: they know what they are supposed to say in church. For many teens, this is just another time to play the great charade, say the right words and get out as quickly as possible. Since you're teaching boundaries as a matter of respect, be sure to show your respect for them. Don't pressure them into making a team or public effort on this subject if you suspect a lack of honesty. Your challenge is to find ways to give them a chance to think honestly about this issue—without pressuring them into saying what you want to hear. It's a matter of respect.

Temptation isn't always thrown at us on inspiration point. Today's key verse says simply that temptation is common; God is faithful; there's always a way out. As teachers, we may be tempted to pressure, to push, to be sure everybody says the right words. But remember that God is faithful. He respects you and the students you teach. He can make a way out of this temptation just a surely as He can keep your young people pure. (Mary Gross, editor, Gospel Light.)

**"Can you please warn people about the dangers of going too far? I speak from experience that emotions get carried away, and you may say and make all the resolutions not to have sex but later it becomes a different story....All the 'in-between' needs to be addressed because it's what leads to sex."—**

Teenage girl,
*Seventeen,* June 1993

SESSION FOUR

BIBLE TUCK-IN™

# HOW FAR IS TOO FAR?

## KEY VERSE

"No temptation has seized you except what is common to man. And God is faithful; he will not let you be tempted beyond what you can bear. But when you are tempted, he will also provide a way out so that you can stand up under it".
1 Corinthians 10:13

## BIBLICAL BASIS

1 Corinthians 10:13; 13:4-7

## THE BIG IDEA

Young people need to set standards before they are in a tempting situation. The decisions they make today will affect them for a lifetime.

## WARM UP (10-15 MINUTES)

### TAKE IT TO THE LIMIT

• Give each student a copy of "Take It to the Limit" on page 63 and a pen or pencil.
• Divide the 10 statements among the students.
• Students survey each other's responses to the statements.
• Students report survey findings to the whole group.

I am someone who would:

| | Yes | Maybe | No. |
|---|---|---|---|
| 1. gamble on the fourth down in a close game | | | |
| 2. rather walk than ride | | | |
| 3. stand up for the underdog | | | |
| 4. go to the bathroom when the movie got scary | | | |
| 5. leave if the game got dull | | | |
| 6. slurp for the last drop | | | |
| 7. rather play sports than eat | | | |
| 8. tell a friend he has bad breath | | | |
| 9. stay in shape the year round | | | |
| 10. buy the first thing I see in a store. | | | |

Fold

---

1. We are called to show each other God's true love. The following description of God's true love is found in 1 Corinthians 13:4-7. All our relationships are to be characterized by these 15 characteristics. Carefully consider the meaning of each characteristic. Then under "Showing True Love," list any acts of affection in a dating relationship that meet the criteria of all 15 characteristics.

Showing True Love:

Love:
is patient
is kind
does not envy
does not boast
is not proud
is not rude
is not self-seeking
is not easily angered
keeps no record of wrongs
does not delight in evil
rejoices in the truth
always protects
always trusts
always hopes
always perseveres

2. Sexual actions are meant to lead to sexual intercourse—one action progressing to another. When you come to the end of your limits, you are often tempted to go beyond. Read 1 Corinthians 10:13. What "way out" does God provide for us in sexual temptation?

(God has given us the Holy Spirit and our consciences to alert us to when we are going beyond God's standards. We have the right and option to say "stop" and flee sin.)

## SO WHAT?

What standards will you establish for your dating life? How can you remember these standards when you are tempted to go too far?

## THINGS TO THINK ABOUT (OPTIONAL)

• Use the questions on page 71 after or as a part of "In the Word."

1. What do you think of the following statement: When a couple is at the point of fondling each other, they tend to lose sight of the other person and focus on their own pleasure?

2. How is sexual temptation different from other kinds of temptation?

3. Linda is 14. She says she is doing everything but having sexual intercourse with her boyfriend. What advice would you give her?

## PARENT PAGE

• Distribute page to parents.

## THE RELATIONSHIP GRAPH

• Give each student a copy of "The Relationship Graph" on page 65 and a pen or pencil, or display the page using an overhead projector.
• As a whole group, read the situations.
• Students individually graph the components of the relationships. As a group, discuss the situations. Then for each component of the relationship, determine the degree of commitment and graph a percentage.

Listed below are two different situations.

1. Bill and Linda have only been dating five weeks, but they are already very involved physically. Linda is a Christian, but she hasn't told Bill because she is afraid that he wouldn't like her. Every time they are together Bill pushes Linda to go farther physically. Linda thinks she loves Bill.

Emotional   Physical   Social   Intellectual   Spiritual   Degree of Commitment

2. Tom and Cara have had a solid friendship for two years. They are active in the church youth group and really enjoy serving on the leadership team. Tom and Cara enjoy long hours of talking together about everything from spiritual life to music. Although they have known each other for a long time, they have just recently become boyfriend and girlfriend. Tom and Cara kissed good-bye after the youth group ski trip.

Emotional   Physical   Social   Intellectual   Spiritual   Degree of Commitment

## TEAM EFFORT—HIGH SCHOOL (15-20 MINUTES)

### HOW FAR SHOULD I GO?

• Give each student a copy of "How Far Should I Go?" on page 67 and a pen or pencil.
• Students individually complete the chart.
• As a whole group, discuss their responses.

We need to set standards *before* we get into a tempting situation. The chart below gives you an opportunity to think about specific actions and to determine the type of relationship in which each one belongs. Consider these actions in light of this question: What would be pleasing to God? And remember, God loves you and wants the very best for you.

Note that the headings range from "Friendship" to "Marriage." At the bottom is a list of abbreviations. Each letter stands for a certain action. Write each letter in the column or columns representing the relationship in which you think that the action would be pleasing to God. For example, "SI" for

"sexual intercourse" has already been placed in the "Marriage" column. We know God's will for intercourse. It is clearly set forth in the Bible. For the other actions listed, thoughtfully and logically determine the standards that will be best for you and glorify God.

| Friendship | Dating | Steady | Engagement | Marriage |
|---|---|---|---|---|
|  |  |  |  | SI |

L = Looking
h = Holding hands
H = Holding hands constantly
HH = Hugging
k = Light kissing
K = Strong kissing
KK = French kissing
B = Fondling the breasts
SO = Fondling the sexual organs
SI = Sexual intercourse

## ON THE WORD (15-20 MINUTES)

### SHOWING TRUE LOVE

• Divide students into groups of three or four. Make sure each group has at least one guy and one girl.
• Display a copy of "Showing True Love" on page 69 using an overhead projector.
• Students complete the Bible study.

# WARM UP

## TAKE IT TO THE LIMIT

I am someone who would:

| | Yes | Maybe | No |
|---|---|---|---|
| 1. gamble on the fourth down in a close game | | | |
| 2. rather walk than ride | | | |
| 3. stand up for the underdog | | | |
| 4. go to the bathroom when the movie got scary | | | |
| 5. leave if the game got dull | | | |
| 6. slurp for the last drop | | | |
| 7. rather play sports than eat | | | |
| 8. tell a friend he has bad breath | | | |
| 9. stay in shape the year round | | | |
| 10. buy the first thing I see in a store. | | | |

## TEAM EFFORT

### THE RELATIONSHIP GRAPH[1]

Listed below are two different situations. As a group, discuss the situations. Then for each component of the relationship, determine the degree of commitment and graph a percentage.

1. Bill and Linda have only been dating five weeks, but they are already very involved physically. Linda is a Christian, but she hasn't told Bill because she is afraid that he wouldn't like her. Every time they are together Bill pushes Linda to go farther physically. Linda thinks she loves Bill.

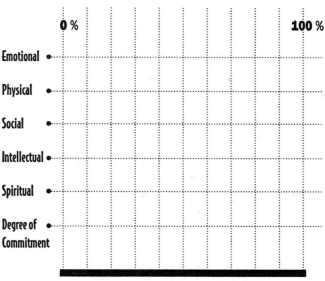

2. Tom and Cara have had a solid friendship for two years. They are active in the church youth group and really enjoy serving on the leadership team. Tom and Cara enjoy long hours of talking together about everything from spiritual life to music. Although they have known each other for a long time, they have just recently become boyfriend and girlfriend. Tom kissed Cara good-bye after the youth group ski trip.

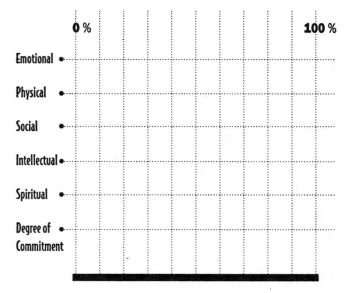

**Note**

1. Chap Clark, *Next Time I Fall In Love* (Grand Rapids, MI: Zondervan, Youth Specialties, 1987), adapted from p. 104. Used by permission.

 **T** EAM EFFORT

## HOW FAR SHOULD I GO?

We need to set standards *before* we get in a tempting situation. The chart below gives you an opportunity to think about specific actions and to determine the type of relationship in which each one belongs. Consider these actions in light of this question: What would be pleasing to God? And remember, God loves you and wants the very best for you.

Note that the headings range from "Friendship" to "Marriage." At the bottom is a list of abbreviations. Each letter stands for a certain action. Write each letter in the column or columns representing the relationship in which you think that the action would be pleasing to God. For example, "SI" for "sexual intercourse" has already been placed in the "Marriage" column. We know God's will for intercourse. It is clearly set forth in the Bible. For the other actions listed, thoughtfully and logically determine the standards that will be best for you and glorify God.

| Friendship | Dating | Steady | Engagement | Marriage |
|---|---|---|---|---|
|  |  |  |  | SI |
|  |  |  |  |  |

L = Looking
h = Holding hands
H = Holding hands constantly
HH = Hugging
k = Light kissing
K = Strong kissing
KK = French kissing
B = Fondling the breasts
SO = Fondling the sexual organs
SI = Sexual intercourse

# IN THE WORD

## SHOWING TRUE LOVE

1. We are called to show each other God's true love. The following description of God's true love is found in 1 Corinthians 13:4-7. All our relationships are to be characterized by these 15 characteristics. Carefully consider the meaning of each characteristic. Then under "Showing True Love," list any acts of affection in a dating relationship that meet the criteria of all 15 characteristics.

Love:

Showing True Love:

is patient

is kind

does not envy

does not boast

is not proud

is not rude

is not self-seeking

is not easily angered

keeps no record of wrongs

does not delight in evil

rejoices in the truth

always protects

always trusts

always hopes

always perseveres

2. Sexual actions are meant to lead to sexual intercourse—one action progressing to another. When you come to the end of your limits, you are often tempted to go beyond. Read 1 Corinthians 10:13. What "way out" does God provide for us in sexual temptation?

# SO WHAT?

What standards will you establish for your dating life? How can you remember these standards when you are tempted to go too far?

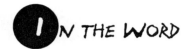

# THINGS TO THINK ABOUT

1. What do you think of the following statement: When a couple is at the point of fondling each other, they tend to lose sight of the other person and focus on their own pleasure?

..............................................................................................................................
..............................................................................................................................
..............................................................................................................................

2. How is sexual temptation different from other kinds of temptation?

..............................................................................................................................
..............................................................................................................................
..............................................................................................................................
..............................................................................................................................

3. Linda is 14. She says she is doing everything but having sexual intercourse with her boyfriend. What advice would you give her?

..............................................................................................................................
..............................................................................................................................
..............................................................................................................................
..............................................................................................................................

# PARENT PAGE

Every normal, red-blooded young person will most likely, at one time or another, come in contact with sexual temptation. As Christians, we know what is best for us, but it is still a struggle. Without God's help, let's face it, we're in trouble! However, we can take some positive steps to overcome sexual temptation.

Here are six positive steps to overcoming sexual temptation. Read these together.

1. **Talk about the problem with your boyfriend or girlfriend.**

   If you do not feel comfortable enough to talk with him or her about your problem, you are definitely going too far and need to seriously consider where your relationship is going to take you.

2. **Set standards.**

   As you get to know your special friend, talk about the standards you would like to set in your relationship. Don't be afraid your friend will think you are a prude. He or she will respect you; if not, is the relationship worth it? Set your standards before you find yourself in the wrong place at the wrong time.

3. **Plan dates that are fun and enjoyable.**

   One of the best ways to overcome sexual temptation is to stay away from "parking spots." Plan dates that allow you to have a lot of fun, including time for good communication.

4. **Pray together.**

   Many Christians find it a great help to pray before a date. This puts the date in a proper perspective and often will remind both of you that, in a very real sense, the Lord goes with you on your dates.

5. **Break up.**

   If you are unable to overcome sexual temptation, it would be wise to break up. At the time you might not feel that there are other guys or girls out there but there are, and some who are better for you. Also, remember a breakup doesn't have to mean forever. Perhaps both of you need some time to redirect your thoughts. At another point in your life you may be able to get back together.

6. **Let God be a part of your dating life.**

   As in all other areas of life, we need the Lord's help and guidance. Invite God on your dates. Let Him lead you and direct you to the right people to date. And memorize 1 Corinthians 10:13.

1. Now that you've read this material what advice would you give to your son or daughter about these suggestions?

2. Read 1 Corinthians 10:13. How does this scriptural principle relate to overcoming sexual temptation?

3. Brainstorm other ideas to keep people from acting upon their sexual temptations.

# DRUGS AND ALCOHOL

## LEADER'S PEP TALK

Let me introduce to you Darlene. (You'll meet her again in Session 5.) This beautiful girl is 14. She is active in church, school and is a good student. Darlene is from a middle-class home where she lives with both parents. By the time Darlene graduates from high school the chances are:

- 88 percent that she will try alcohol
- 57 percent that she will try an illicit drug
- 33 percent that she will smoke marijuana on occasion
- 33 percent that she will get drunk once a month
- 1 in 6 that she will try cocaine or crack.

It's not like it used to be when we were in junior and senior high school. Sure we were 11, 13, 16 and 18, but we were never their age. They experience so much at such an early age. Today 39 percent of all fifth graders report pressure to drink, and 68 percent of all eighth graders report pressure to drink.

The mistake some of us have made is that we believe only bad teens use drugs and abuse alcohol. Wrong. Most young people will experience it but the ones who develop a problem are the ones who don't understand the powerful affect of drugs and alcohol on the personhood.

### WHY DO TEENS ABUSE DRUGS AND ALCOHOL?

Drugs and alcohol provide a false sense of relief, but most of the time they deaden a young person's pain. Second, drugs and alcohol are so appealing to students (and adults) because they work every time. Drugs and alcohol are dependable while family and friends unfortunately are not always dependable. If a young person is worried about family struggles, grades, loss of a boyfriend or girlfriend or whatever problem, the drugs or alcohol can be counted on to make hurt go away temporarily. It's this simple: Drugs make them feel good, and drugs work. These two facts are absolutely pertinent to understanding the incredible draw, by so many, toward harmful dependency and addiction.

### WHAT HAPPENS WHEN TEENS USE DRUGS AND ALCOHOL?

1. **They stop learning how to cope properly with the stress.** At whatever age they started putting a chemical inside them to deaden their pain, they stopped learning how to cope properly with stress. It's easy to detox an alcoholic or drug user. The more difficult part is to reteach them how to deal with their problems in a different way than drinking or using drugs.

2. **Young people change in stages.** No one takes a drink of their first beer and instantly becomes addicted. It's important for youth workers to know the stages in order to help with prevention.

Stage 1:   Experimental Stage

Stage 2:   Social Use Stage
   • move to more regular use with a higher tolerance

Stage 3:   Dependency
   • often a daily preoccupation
   • use of harder drugs and alcohol, higher number of times a week
   • changes in behavior—often subtle
   • school grades often fall and laziness becomes evident

Stage 4:   Addiction—harmful dependency
   • preoccupation with getting high
   • loss of control
   • violate their value system
   • often move from one peer group to another

Now this is where you come into the picture. One of the most effective ways to help students with the issue of drug and alcohol abuse, besides good parenting, is when teens get the chance to be educated and talk about this important part of their life. As you enter the next four sessions you will, no doubt, have students at every stage and some who are just deciding what to do about their use of alcohol and drugs. In these sessions you have a good opportunity to help your young people make wise decisions, and prevent an incredible amount of pain in life by educating them about drugs and alcohol.

As you do this, keep in mind this Scripture: "Do you not know that your body is a temple of the Holy Spirit, who is in you, whom you have received from God? You are not your own; you were bought at a price. Therefore honor God with your body" (1 Corinthians 6:19).

You have the opportunity to educate, challenge and encourage teens to look at what they are doing to their temple when they put a negative substance into their body. You will help them see just how it affects their life and their spiritual life.

Are you ready? Buckle you seat belt and hang on because you may be in for a wild ride. And thanks for being there for your students. You may be the only significant adult they can talk to about this serious issue.

# DRUGS AT YOUR DOORSTEP

## **K**EY VERSE

"**W**ine is a mocker and beer a brawler; whoever is led astray by them is not wise." Proverbs 20:1.

## **B**IBLICAL BASIS

**P**roverbs 20:1; 23:29-35
**I**saiah 5:11,12

## **T**HE BIG IDEA

**Y**oung people are more susceptible to drug and alcohol abuse than they realize.

## **A**IMS OF THIS SESSION

**D**uring this session you will guide students to:
* Examine how susceptible they are to drug and alcohol abuse;
* Discover educational truths about drug and alcohol abuse;
* Evaluate their feelings on drug and alcohol use.

## **W**ARM UP

### JUST ONE QUESTION—
An opportunity for teens to get to know each other one-on-one.

## **T**EAM EFFORT— JUNIOR HIGH/ MIDDLE SCHOOL

### MEET DARLENE—
A look at an average student's experience with drugs and alcohol.

## **T**EAM EFFORT— HIGH SCHOOL

### ALCOHOL, ALCOHOLISM AND ME—
A quiz of teens' knowledge of alcohol and alcoholism.

## **I**N THE WORD

### JESUS MEETS THE PRESS—
A Bible study on God's teaching on the use of drugs and alcohol.

## **T**HINGS TO THINK ABOUT (OPTIONAL)

**Q**uestions to get teens thinking and talking about drug and alcohol use among young people.

## **P**ARENT PAGE

**A** tool to get the session into the home and allow parents and teens to discuss drug and alcohol use among young people.

## LEADER'S DEVOTIONAL

Drug and alcohol use and abuse are not new. From the days of the Whiskey Rebellion through the hard-drinking old west into the opium smoking 1890s, people have always had something available to them to "forget their troubles." The psychedelic 1960s had been preceded by prescription-drug abuse and the availability of heroin and marijuana. Even during the era of Prohibition, the availability of alcohol was an ironic joke. Coping with life's problems by dropping out, turning on or tuning out has always been available in one form or another.

So why the concern about drug and alcohol abuse today? The temptations aren't new. They're common. It's partly a matter of greater availability. It's also a matter of greater pressure. But the bottom line is this: Our students live and move in a society where adults (through everything from pop songs to movies, but mainly through personal example) are not teaching them *any* methods of dealing with problems other than walking away, getting drunk or getting stoned.

Your challenge is not just to educate. It goes beyond exhorting teens to keep the temple of the Holy Spirit clean and usable. Even more vital is to prove—by your life—what it means to have a body that is God's temple. You must show—by your responses to problems—biblical ways to deal with trouble. Then you'll really be helping your teens. Once they understand the ways Christians can solve problems, when they see they have the resources to deal with trouble, when they know where they can go for real help—the world's shoddy methods of dealing with trouble and pain will be shown up for what they are. Never forget what an effective method of teaching it is: Jesus left us an example that we should follow in His steps. Give your young people the gift of your example. (Mary Gross, editor, Gospel Light.)

**"I don't consider (marijuana) a drug. It's a plant. Coke. I don't do that.... That's a drug."—**

Teenage boy,
*Newsweek*,
November 1, 1993

SESSION FIVE

BIBLE TUCK-IN ™

# DRUGS AT YOUR DOORSTEP

## Key Verse

"Wine is a mocker and beer a brawler; whoever is led astray by them is not wise." Proverbs 20:1

## Biblical Basis

Proverbs 20:1; 23:29-35; Isaiah 5:11,12

## The Big Idea

Young people are more susceptible to drug and alcohol abuse than they realize.

## Warm Up (5-10 Minutes)

### Just One Question

- Divide students into pairs.
- Read aloud the following statements.
- Students complete the statement to their partners.

If I could ask God just one question I would ask...

The thing that gives me greatest satisfaction is...

The thing that causes me greatest concern is...

--- Fold ---

79

## On the Word (25-30 Minutes)

### Jesus Meets the Press

- Divide students into groups of three or four.
- Give each student a copy of "Jesus Meets the Press" on page 85 and a pen or pencil, or display the page using an overhead projector.
- Students complete Bible study.
- Students share interview scripts.

Imagine Jesus on a Jerusalem news interview. The topic is drug and alcohol use and abuse among teenagers at Jerusalem High School. Although Jesus obviously did not speak specifically about the drugs and alcohol problem at Jerusalem High School, He did share principles that might pertain to this situation. Jesus also obviously had access to the teaching of the Old Testament.

Write out an interview script between Jesus and a reporter. The reporter asks the questions, and Jesus answers based on the principles found in Proverbs 20:1; 23:29-35; Isaiah 5:11,12 and common sense. What are your thoughts on the subject?

1. Reporter: It seems like most of today's young people are drinking and using drugs. What are your thoughts on the subject?

2. Reporter: What about teens just using the easy stuff like beer and wine coolers?

3. Reporter: If you were at a party where the alcohol and drugs were free flowing, what would you do?

4. Reporter: Can you walk with God and continue getting high?

5. Reporter: What policies would you develop on alcohol and drug use among young people?

## So What?

What new information did you learn about drugs and alcohol? How does that change your feelings about drug and alcohol use?

## Things to Think About (Optional)

- Use the questions on page 87 after or as a part of "In the Word."

1. Describe the drug and alcohol problem at your school. At your church.

2. Why do you think teens drink and use drugs?

3. What are your fears for your friends who drink or use drugs?

## Parent Page

- Distribute page to parents.

### Note

1. Barbara R. Lorch and Robert H. Hughes, "Church Youth, Alcohol and Drug Education Programs and Youth Substance Use," *Journal of Alcohol and Drug Education*, Vol. 33, No. 2 (Winter 1988): 15.

# TEAM EFFORT—JUNIOR HIGH/MIDDLE SCHOOL (15-20 MINUTES)

## MEET DARLENE

- Divide students into groups of three or four.
- Display a copy of "Meet Darlene?" on page 81 using an overhead projector.
- Read aloud the situation and statements.
- Each group tries to guess the correct percent for each statement.
- As a whole group discuss the questions.

Darlene is 14 years old. She is a very attractive girl who is active in school and gets good grades. Darlene is also a youth group leader at the church she attends with her mom, dad and two brothers. What are the chances that Darlene will have these experiences with drugs and alcohol?

............ percent chance she will try alcohol.

(Eighty-seven percent chance she will try alcohol.)

............ percent chance she will try an illicit drug.

(Fifty-six percent chance she will try an illicit drug.)

............ percent chance she will smoke marijuana on occasion.

(Thirty-three percent chance she will smoke marijuana on occasion.)

............ percent chance she will smoke marijuana regularly.

(Twenty-five percent chance she will smoke marijuana regularly.)

............ percent chance she will try cocaine or crack.

(Seventeen percent chance she will try cocaine or crack.[1])

**1. What are your feelings when confronted with those statistics?**

**2. These statistics are on a national level. How do they differ from the statistics for your school?**

# TEAM EFFORT—HIGH SCHOOL (15-20 MINUTES)

## ALCOHOL, ALCOHOLISM AND ME

- Divide students into groups of three or four.
- Display a copy of "Alcohol, Alcoholism and Me" on page 83 using an overhead projector.
- Read aloud the question.
- Each group tries to guess the correct answer.
- As a whole group, discuss the answers.

**Circle the letter of the correct answer.**

Fold

**1. Heavy drinking of alcohol over a long time can cause damage to:**

a. the brain
b. the liver
c. the heart
d. a, b and c.

(D. Alcohol can kill cells and weaken these organs.)

**2. The number one drug problem among young people is:**

a. crack
b. alcohol
c. tobacco.

(B. More than half of all junior and senior high school students have tried alcohol.)

**3. Which of the following has as much alcohol as 1 ounce of whiskey?**

a. 12 oz. beer
b. 8 oz. glass of wine
c. 12 oz. wine cooler
d. a, b and c.

(D. Each has about the same amount of alcohol.)

**4. Write T for true or F for false before each statement.**

a. ........ Alcoholism is the same as being drunk.

(False. A person can drink and get drunk but not be an alcoholic.)

b. ........ A person who is an alcoholic can control the urge to drink.

(False. An alcoholic is not in control of his or her drinking.)

c. ........ After drinking, people often say or do things they wouldn't normally say or do.

(True. As a person drinks more and more, he or she loses control of some faculties.)

d. ........ Alcohol is a drug.

(True. A drug is a psychoactive substance that speeds up or slows down a person's body. Alcohol slows it down.)

e. ........ Long-term alcohol abuse can shorten a person's life.

(True. Long-term drinking can cause fatal diseases.)

f. ........ A child of an alcoholic parent is less likely to abuse alcohol.

(False. Alcoholism tends to run in families.)

**5. What are two ways alcohol affects the body?**

Write your answer after each question.

(Alcohol slows down a person's brain and bodily control.)

**6. What are two of the main reasons that young people drink alcohol?**

(Peer pressure; to declare their independence; to have more fun; they are lonely; to reduce anxiety and fear; etc.)

## TEAM EFFORT

### MEET DARLENE

Darlene is 14 years old. She is a very attractive girl who is active in school and gets good grades. Darlene is also a youth group leader at the church she attends with her mom, dad and two brothers. What are the chances that Darlene will have these experiences with drugs and alcohol?

........... percent chance she will try alcohol.

........... percent chance she will try an illicit drug.

........... percent chance she will smoke marijuana on occasion.

........... percent chance she will smoke marijuana regularly.

........... percent chance she will try cocaine or crack.

**1.** What are your feelings when confronted with those statistics?

........................................................................................................................

........................................................................................................................

........................................................................................................................

**2.** These statistics are on a national level. How do they differ from the statistics for your school?

........................................................................................................................

........................................................................................................................

........................................................................................................................

........................................................................................................................

# TEAM EFFORT

## ALCOHOL, ALCOHOLISM AND ME

Circle the letter of the correct answer.

**1.** Heavy drinking of alcohol over a long time can cause damage to:

a. the brain

b. the liver

c. the heart

d. a, b and c.

**2.** The number one drug problem among young people is:

a. crack

b. alcohol

c. tobacco.

**3.** Which of the following has as much alcohol as 1 ounce of whiskey?

a. 12 oz. beer

b. 8 oz. glass of wine

c. 12 oz. wine cooler

d. a, b and c.

**4.** Write *T* for true or *F* for false before each statement.

a......... Alcoholism is the same as being drunk.

b......... A person who is an alcoholic can control the urge to drink.

c......... After drinking, people often say or do things they wouldn't normally say or do.

d......... Alcohol is a drug.

e......... Long-term alcohol abuse can shorten a person's life.

f......... A child of an alcoholic parent is less likely to abuse alcohol.

Write your answer after each question.

**5.** What are two ways alcohol affects the body?

...................................................................................................................................

...................................................................................................................................

...................................................................................................................................

**6.** What are two of the main reasons that young people drink alcohol?

...................................................................................................................................

...................................................................................................................................

83

# IN THE WORD

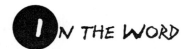

## JESUS MEETS THE PRESS

Imagine Jesus on a Jerusalem news interview. The topic is drug and alcohol use and abuse among teenagers at Jerusalem High School. Although Jesus obviously did not speak specifically about the drugs and alcohol problem at Jerusalem High School, He did share principles that might pertain to this situation. Jesus also obviously had access to the teaching of the Old Testament.

Write out an interview script between Jesus and a reporter. The reporter asks the questions, and Jesus answers based on the principles found in Proverbs 20:1; 23:29-35; Isaiah 5:11,12 and common sense.

**1.** Reporter: It seems like most of today's young people are drinking and using drugs. What are your thoughts on the subject?

.................................................................................................................

.................................................................................................................

.................................................................................................................

**2.** Reporter: What about teens just using the easy stuff like beer and wine coolers?

.................................................................................................................

.................................................................................................................

.................................................................................................................

**3.** Reporter: If you were at a party where the alcohol and drugs were free flowing, what would you do?

.................................................................................................................

.................................................................................................................

.................................................................................................................

**4.** Reporter: Can you walk with God and continue getting high?

.................................................................................................................

.................................................................................................................

.................................................................................................................

**5.** Reporter: What policies would you develop on alcohol and drug use among young people?

.................................................................................................................

.................................................................................................................

.................................................................................................................

.................................................................................................................

.................................................................................................................

## SO WHAT?

What new information did you learn about drugs and alcohol? How does that change your feelings about drug and alcohol use?

.................................................................................................................

.................................................................................................................

.................................................................................................................

.................................................................................................................

.................................................................................................................

# Things to Think About

**1.** Describe the drug and alcohol problem at your school. At your church.

.................................................................................................
.................................................................................................
.................................................................................................

**2.** Why do you think teens drink and use drugs?

.................................................................................................
.................................................................................................
.................................................................................................
.................................................................................................

**3.** What are your fears for your friends who drink or use drugs?

.................................................................................................
.................................................................................................
.................................................................................................

# PARENT PAGE

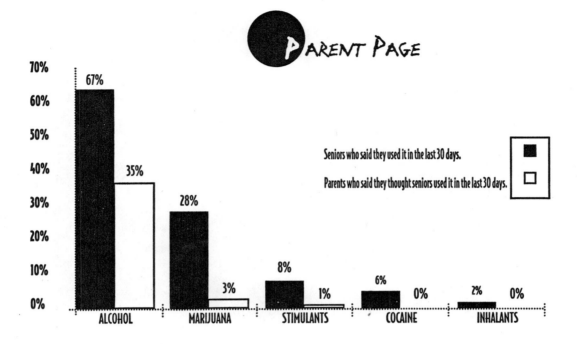

Seniors who said they used it in the last 30 days. ■

Parents who said they thought seniors used it in the last 30 days. □

## PARENTS UNDERESTIMATE DRUG USAGE[2]

According to an Emory University School of Medicine survey, parents underestimate their kids' drug and alcohol use. The researchers asked 402 seniors if they had used various substances in the last 30 days. Parents were asked if they thought the seniors had used the same substances in the last 30 days. Parents estimated alcohol and drug usage consistently lower than actual senior usage.

**I.** Why do you think parents underestimate the use of drugs and alcohol with their children?

.................................................................................................................

.................................................................................................................

.................................................................................................................

**2.** What is our family's policy on drug and alcohol use and abuse?

.................................................................................................................

.................................................................................................................

.................................................................................................................

**3.** Read Proverbs 20:1. How does this affect our family's policy on drug and alcohol use and abuse?

.................................................................................................................

....................................................................................    ..........................

**Session 5 "Drugs at Your Doorstep" Date**..........................

**Note**

2. Steve Arterburn and Jim Burns, *Drug Proof Your Kids* (Colorado Springs, CO: Focus on the Family, 1989), p. 108. Used by permission.

# WHAT HAPPENS WHEN YOU USE DRUGS AND ALCOHOL?

## KEY VERSE

"I put this in human terms because you are weak in your natural selves. Just as you used to offer the parts of your body in slavery to impurity and to ever-increasing wickedness, so now offer them in slavery to righteousness." Romans 6:19

## BIBLICAL BASIS

Luke 10:27
Romans 6:19
1 Corinthians 6:19,20; 9:26,27
2 Corinthians 4:10,11
1 Thessalonians 5:23

## THE BIG IDEA

Drugs and alcohol can have dangerous effects on the body. Teens are to honor God with their bodies.

## AIMS OF THIS SESSION

During this session you will guide students to:

• Examine the effects of drugs and alcohol on their bodies;

• Discover God's intent for their bodies;

• Take action to honor God with their bodies.

## WARM UP

**FEELING GOOD ALL OVER—**
Young people share the good that is happening in their lives.

## TEAM EFFORT— JUNIOR HIGH/ MIDDLE SCHOOL

**MEET DARLENE—**
A look at an average student's experience with drugs and alcohol.

## TEAM EFFORT— HIGH SCHOOL

**ALCOHOL, ALCOHOLISM AND ME—**
A quiz of teens' knowledge of alcohol and alcoholism.

## IN THE WORD

**HONORING GOD WITH YOUR BODY—**
A Bible study on what the body of a Christian looks like.

## THINGS TO THINK ABOUT (OPTIONAL)

Questions to get teens thinking and talking about the effects of drug and alcohol use.

## PARENT PAGE

A tool to get the session into the home and allow parents and teens to discuss the stages of drug use and dependency.

## LEADER'S DEVOTIONAL

As you are well aware, when you stand in front of teens for any length of time, they pick up on everything about you. They know what really gets to you, they know how sincere you are and probably what your shoe size is.

Then the time comes when a young person needs to talk. You may well be the only adult a teen knows who seems open. But what will you say to the student who comes to you and wants to tell you about his or her drug or alcohol problem? Of course, the teen will already know whether you are really interested and available. (That was pegged the first time he or she sat in your class.) But he or she may be terrified of your responses.

So what is a proper response? Are you going to turn the student in to the authorities? Tell his or her parents? How much confidentiality will you keep? Will you somehow give him or her the impression that it's okay to cover this up? Will you call in another counselor?

The answers aren't going to be provided here! There are no pat answers because these aren't pat questions. But what this does point out is the need for *prayerful* reactions. Don't wait for that young person to take you by surprise. Start now to pray earnestly! Part of the challenge for you is to provide a safe place where teens who do need help can come without fear. Ask God to literally give you the facial expressions, the voice, the control you need to let a student talk freely. Your job is not to condone but you must listen without judging until the problem is all laid out. Why? Because your reaction is the first step in recovery for the teen who comes to you. He or she is already not handling life's problems well. Your response is a living lesson in how to deal with this problem he or she has brought without blowing up, giving up, turning on or getting drunk. You'll teach a great deal just by what you show.

You'll need God's help for proper reactions, wisdom and words. And He will give you all you need for this delicate task. Don't fail to ask Him! (Mary Gross, editor, Gospel Light.)

**"The first time we tried the vocal on 'Alcohol,' he was too drunk to sing it. That's rather poetic."—**

Gibby Haynes, musician,
*Musician*, March 1993

# WHAT HAPPENS WHEN YOU USE
# DRUGS AND ALCOHOL?

## KEY VERSE

"I put this in human terms because you are weak in your natural selves. Just as you used to offer the parts of your body in slavery to impurity and to ever-increasing wickedness, so now offer them in slavery to righteousness."
Romans 6:19

## BIBLICAL BASIS

Luke 10:27; Romans 6:19; 1 Corinthians 6:19,20; 9:26,27; 2 Corinthians 4:10,11; 1 Thessalonians 5:23

## THE BIG IDEA

Drugs and alcohol can have dangerous effects on the body. Teens are to honor God with their bodies.

## WARM UP (5-10 MINUTES)

### FEELING GOOD ALL OVER

• Give each student a copy of "Feeling Good All Over" on page 95 and a pen or pencil.
• Students individually complete page.
• As a whole group, share responses.
In the first column list three things you do that make you feel good.
In the second column list three things you do to make others feel good.
In the third column list three things others do that make you feel good.
In the fourth column list three things Christ is doing in your life that make you feel good.

| Toward Self | Toward Others | From Others | From Christ |
| --- | --- | --- | --- |
| 1. | | | |
| 2. | | | |
| 3. | | | |

---- Fold ----

**93**

---

2. Now describe the body of a Christian.

3. How does this person differ from a person who uses drugs and alcohol?

## SO WHAT?

How are you doing in honoring God with your body? (Consider drugs, alcohol, food, exercise, sleep, etc.) What one thing can you do to honor God with your body?

## THINGS TO THINK ABOUT (OPTIONAL)

• Use the questions on page 101 after or as a part of "In the Word."
1. How does peer pressure or the pressure to conform relate to drug and alcohol use?

How does a low self-image relate to drug and alcohol use?

2. If you saw yourself sinking into having problems with drugs or alcohol, who would you go to for help?

3. Discuss the addictive nature of drugs and alcohol.

## PARENT PAGE

• Distribute page to parents.

# TEAM EFFORT—JUNIOR HIGH/ MIDDLE SCHOOL (15-20 MINUTES)

## THE MYTH

- Display a copy of "The Myth" on page 95 using an overhead projector.
- As a whole group, discuss the questions.

1. Look at the picture of the sober beauty queen. Now look again. (Turn picture upside down.) Many people don't want to think about the harmful effects of drug and alcohol abuse. What do you see?

2. How can this be a word picture of what happens to many who choose to use and abuse drugs or alcohol?

3. Share stories of either famous people or others you know (without using their names) who have crashed and burned because of drug or alcohol use and abuse. How did drugs or alcohol affect their careers, relationships and health?
(Be prepared to share examples and/or suggest famous people.)

# TEAM EFFORT—HIGH SCHOOL (15-20 MINUTES)

## JERRY—A CASE STUDY

- Give each student a copy of "Jerry—A Case Study" on page 97 and a pen or pencil, or display the page using an overhead projector.
- As a whole group, read aloud the case study and discuss the questions.

Jerry is a great person. He is doing well as a pitcher on the varsity baseball team and is well liked by his peers. Jerry's funny personality leads him to be very popular and makes him the class clown.

Lately you've smelled alcohol on Jerry's breath and heard rumors he has been using marijuana.

So far it really hasn't affected his athletics. His grades have slipped a little, but he definitely isn't flunking out. As one of Jerry's best friends you've noticed some subtle changes in his behavior. He's not as friendly when he has beer on his breath. He is getting a little more free with his language, and he hangs out with girls who have a reputation for being "loose" with their morals. You know it's been a hard year because his mom and alcoholic dad finally split up after several really rough years.

1. What are all the issues affecting Jerry's life?

2. What can you do to be a good friend to Jerry?

3. What advice would you give Jerry about his actions?

4. Remember: Drugs and alcohol make you feel good. They deaden your pain. But how can these statements be only "half-truths"?

5. How do these "half-truths" relate to Jerry's life?

6. What are other reasons, both positive and negative, young people use drugs and alcohol?

Fold

# IN THE WORD (20-25 MINUTES)

## HONORING GOD WITH YOUR BODY

- Divide students into groups of three or four.
- Give each student a copy of "Honoring God with Your Body" on page 99 and a pen or pencil.
- Students complete the Bible study.
- Students share illustrations.

1. Read the following Scriptures. How do they describe the body of a Christian?

Luke 10:27
(We are to love God with our bodies.)

Romans 6:19
(Our bodies are to obey righteousness and lead to holiness.)

1 Corinthians 6:19,20
(God lives within our bodies.)

1 Corinthians 9:26,27
(We are to discipline and control our bodies.)

2 Corinthians 4:10,11
(Our bodies show God's presence in our lives.)

1 Thessalonians 5:23
(God can keep our bodies blameless.)

# WARM UP

## FEELING GOOD ALL OVER

In the first column list three things you do that make you feel good.
In the second column list three things you do to make others feel good.
In the third column list three things others do that make you feel good.
In the fourth column list three things Christ is doing in your life that make
you feel good.

| | Toward Self | Toward Others | From Others | From Christ |
|---|---|---|---|---|
| **1.** | | | | |
| **2.** | | | | |
| **3.** | | | | |

# TEAM EFFORT

## THE MYTH

Many people don't want to think about the harmful effects of
drug and alcohol abuse.

**1.** Look at the picture of the sober beauty queen. Now look again. What do you see?

........................................................................................................

........................................................................................................

**2.** How can this be a word picture of what happens to many who choose to use and abuse
drugs or alcohol?

........................................................................................................

........................................................................................................

**3.** Share stories of either famous people or others you know (without using their names) who have
crashed and burned because of drug or alcohol use and abuse. How did drugs or alcohol affect their
careers, relationships and health?

........................................................................................................

........................................................................................................

........................................................................................................

**BEFORE 6 BEERS**

**AFTER 6 BEERS**

## Team Effort

### JERRY—A CASE STUDY

Jerry is a great person. He is doing well as a pitcher on the varsity baseball team and is well liked by his peers. Jerry's funny personality leads him to be very popular and makes him the class clown.

Lately you've smelled alcohol on Jerry's breath and heard rumors he has been using marijuana. So far it really hasn't affected his athletics. His grades have slipped a little, but he definitely isn't flunking out. As one of Jerry's best friends you've noticed some subtle changes in his behavior. He's not as friendly when he has beer on his breath. He is getting a little more free with his language, and he hangs out with girls who have a reputation for being "loose" with their morals. You know it's been a hard year because his mom and alcoholic dad finally split up after several really rough years.

**1.** What are all the issues affecting Jerry's life?

...................................................................................................................

...................................................................................................................

**2.** What can you do to be a good friend to Jerry?

...................................................................................................................

...................................................................................................................

**3.** What advice would you give Jerry about his actions?

...................................................................................................................

...................................................................................................................

**4.** Remember: Drugs and alcohol make you feel good. They deaden your pain. But how can these statements be only "half-truths"?

...................................................................................................................

...................................................................................................................

**5.** How do these "half-truths" relate to Jerry's life?

...................................................................................................................

...................................................................................................................

**6.** What are other reasons, both positive and negative, young people use drugs and alcohol?

...................................................................................................................

...................................................................................................................

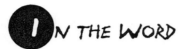

# IN THE WORD

## HONORING GOD WITH YOUR BODY

**1. Read the following Scriptures. How do they describe the body of a Christian?**

Luke 10:27

Romans 6:19

1 Corinthians 6:19,20

1 Corinthians 9:26,27

2 Corinthians 4:10,11

1 Thessalonians 5:23

**2. Now describe the body of a Christian.**

**3. How does this person differ from a person who uses drugs and alcohol?**

## SO WHAT?

How are you doing in honoring God with your body? (Consider drugs, alcohol, food, exercise, sleep, etc.) What one thing can you do to honor God with your body?

# Things to Think About

**1.** How does peer pressure or the pressure to conform relate to drug and alcohol use? How does a low self-image relate to drug and alcohol use?

.............................................................................................................................

.............................................................................................................................

.............................................................................................................................

**2.** If you saw yourself sinking into having problems with drugs or alcohol, who would you go to for help?

.............................................................................................................................

.............................................................................................................................

.............................................................................................................................

**3.** Discuss the addictive nature of drugs and alcohol.

.............................................................................................................................

.............................................................................................................................

.............................................................................................................................

.............................................................................................................................

# PARENT PAGE

## WHAT HAPPENS WHEN PEOPLE USE DRUGS AND ALCOHOL?

**1. Together read the following information.**

- People stop learning how to cope with stress properly. At whatever age they started putting a chemical into their systems to make them feel good and deaden their pain, that is the age at which they quit coping with stress properly.

- People change in four stages.

  a. Start with experimental stage

  b. Move to social use stage—This leads to regular use with a high tolerance for drugs.

  c. Move to dependency (daily preoccupation)—This includes use of harder drugs, a higher usage per week and changes in behavior such as getting lazy and letting grades drop

  d. Move to addiction (harmful dependency)—This includes preoccupation with getting high, loss of control, violation of their value systems and moving from one peer group to another.

**2. What new information did you learn?**

..................................................................................................................................

..................................................................................................................................

..................................................................................................................................

**3. What are the most important things to remember in the above information?**

..................................................................................................................................

..................................................................................................................................

..................................................................................................................................

**4. With this new information, what decisions should we make about drug and alcohol use?**

..................................................................................................................................

..................................................................................................................................

..................................................................................................................................

..................................................................................................................................

Session 6 "What Happens When You Use
Drugs and Alcohol?" Date..........................

# THE FIGHT FOR CONTROL

## EY VERSE

"Do not get drunk on wine, which leads to debauchery. Instead, be filled with the Spirit."
Ephesians 5:18

## IBLICAL BASIS

Romans 8:5-8;
1 Corinthians 6:12;
Ephesians 5:18;
Colossians 3:17; 1 Peter 4:7;
2 Peter 1:5-9

## THE BIG IDEA

When making a choice to use or not use drugs or alcohol, teens need to first ask, "Who's in control?"

## AIMS OF THIS SESSION

During this session you will guide students to:

- Examine the various choices they can make about using drugs and alcohol;
- Discover biblical guidelines on alcohol and drug use;
- Develop a philosophy and guidelines for drug and alcohol use.

## WARM UP

**Think Through Your Actions—**
A look at possible detrimental effects of drug and alcohol use.

## TEAM EFFORT— JUNIOR HIGH/ MIDDLE SCHOOL

**The Balloon Tribe—**
A story that presents possible choices for drug and alcohol use.

## TEAM EFFORT— HIGH SCHOOL

**"Just Say No" Game—**
Role plays of drug and alcohol offers.

## IN THE WORD

**Who's in Control?—**
A Bible study on being self-controlled and in step with the Holy Spirit.

## THINGS TO THINK ABOUT (OPTIONAL)

Questions to get teens thinking and talking about using drugs and alcohol.

## PARENT PAGE

A tool to get the session into the home and allow parents and teens to discuss their choices in using drugs and alcohol.

## LEADER'S DEVOTIONAL

Some young people are aiming for the top. He wants to play professional basketball. She wants to become a gymnast. These teens know what discipline is about. They've sacrificed to gain the goal they are seeking. These teens usually have already said no to drugs and alcohol simply because that would keep them from their goal of peak physical performance.

But maybe you don't have a group of motivated athletes before you. Maybe they're just normal students who like to do a lot of things but don't have a driving ambition for physical perfection. What can you tell them about balancing their lives and disciplining themselves to avoid drugs and alcohol?

Drug and alcohol use is a symptom. If a teen feels like he or she isn't going anywhere in life, isn't driven and motivated by something, drug and alcohol use can end boredom, make a person feel better and certainly can motivate someone—although not to desirable behavior!

So what's the answer? A big physical fitness program? No. We have the very best motivator, the kind that can spur students on to self-discipline. It's the antidote to boredom, to aimlessness, to feeling like they aren't going anywhere! And it's just this simple: When young people begin to understand that *God* thinks they are important and wants to see them be all He has made them to be, when they realize He has *important* plans for each of them, then discipline, saying no, begins to make sense.

Share with your students the wonder and excitement of the big plans God has for each of their lives! And don't keep this on the theoretical level. Tell them about the exciting ways God has revealed His plans for your life and the lives of others right around you. God's always got something infinitely better than the glitter Satan flashes before our eyes. Give your teens the vision of their amazing value to God, His big plans for each of them and the excitement of knowing what He is up to! (Mary Gross, editor, Gospel Light.)

**"The River Phoenix image was pure but I guess he wasn't. He betrayed his image."—**

Teenage boy on the drug-caused death of actor River Phoenix, *Time*, November 15, 1993

# THE FIGHT FOR CONTROL

## K EY VERSE

"Do not get drunk on wine, which leads to debauchery. Instead, be filled with the Spirit." Ephesians 5:18

## B IBLICAL BASIS

Romans 8:5-8; 1 Corinthians 6:12; Ephesians 5:18; Colossians 3:17; 1 Peter 4:7; 2 Peter 1:5-9

## T HE BIG IDEA

When making a choice to use or not use drugs or alcohol, teens need to first ask, "Who's in control?"

## W ARM UP (5-7 MINUTES)
### THINK THROUGH YOUR ACTIONS

- Divide students into groups of three or four.
- Provide pencil or pen and paper for someone in each group to write a list.
- Students list as many situations as they can where people could get themselves into trouble because they are drunk or high.
- After approximately two minutes find out which group wrote the most situations.
- Ask each group to share some situations.

---- Fold ----

107

---

2 Peter 1:5-9

...People should never touch the stuff.

...People should be able to use alcohol, but not in excess.

...People have the right to use alcohol as much as they want.

1. Do you think a person can be controlled by the Holy Spirit and get drunk or high at the same time? Why or why not?

...................................................

...................................................

2. Do you think that most teenagers are able to control drinking and/or drugs? Why or why not?

...................................................

...................................................

3. How would a person know if he or she had passed the point of being in control?

...................................................

...................................................

## S O WHAT?

Write out your philosophy and guidelines for drug and alcohol use.

## T HINGS TO THINK ABOUT (OPTIONAL)

- Use the questions on page 115 after or as a part of "In the Word."

1. Is using drugs or drinking necessarily a "Christian" issue? Why or why not?

...................................................

2. Should you attend a party where you know drugs and drinking will be prevalent? Why or why not?

...................................................

...................................................

3. Should a Christian drink socially? Where would you draw the line?

...................................................

## P ARENT PAGE

- Distribute page to parents.

# TEAM EFFORT—JUNIOR HIGH/MIDDLE SCHOOL (15-20 MINUTES)

## THE BALLOON TRIBE

- Divide students into Group One, Group Two and Group Three. If the three groups are too large, divide them into six or nine groups.
- Give each student a copy of "The Balloon Tribe" on page 109, or display a copy using an overhead projector.
- Read aloud the story.
- Assign a position to each group.
- Students defend their positions.

Group One: Blowing up balloons is fine, and it's okay to run out of breath and get dizzy if you feel like it.

Group Two: Occasional balloon blowing is okay, but it's morally wrong to get dizzy.

Group Three: Blowing up balloons is wrong at all times.

# TEAM EFFORT—HIGH SCHOOL (15-20 MINUTES)

## "JUST SAY NO" GAME

- Give each student a copy of "Just Say No' Game" on page 111 and a pen or pencil, or display the page using an overhead projector.
- Divide students into pairs.
- Assign each pair a situation to role-play. Remind them the goal is to give a realistic response, not to glamorize drug and alcohol use.
- Students state the positions they chose and perform role plays.

Role-play your situation from one of three positions: using drugs and alcohol is always okay, using drugs and alcohol is occasionally okay or using drugs and alcohol is always wrong.

Alcohol Offers:

1. Your sister and her friend pick you up from a party, and his friend offers you a cold beer for the trip home.

2. At a party, the gang gets into the parents' liquor cabinet. Everyone starts drinking out of a bottle of vodka.

3. Your parents take you out to a nice dinner at a local club. Your dad orders everyone something to drink and tells you it's okay for you to have one.

4. On a fishing trip, you go up the river with your brother. You are in the middle of the forest, and he says that since no one is around you can have a beer.

Drug Offers:

1. You are at school, between classes, and someone asks you to walk into the bathroom to smoke a joint.

2. A boy you know says he snuck some of his mother's tranquilizers out of the medicine cabinet. He asks you to meet him after school to take them.

3. One of the local hangouts, a friend says she has some bottles of cough syrup. If you drink it, she promises you will feel as though you are in another world.

4. At one of the high school seniors offers to give you a ride home and tells you he has some crack that is pure and expensive.

# IN THE WORD (25-33 MINUTES)

## WHO'S IN CONTROL?

- Give each student a copy of "Who's in Control?" on page 113 and a pen or pencil.
- Students individually complete the Bible study.
- As a whole group, discuss the questions.

Read the following Scriptures. Check the position that is supported by each Scripture.

Romans 8:5-8
...People should never touch the stuff.
...People should be able to use alcohol, but not in excess.
...People have the right to use alcohol as much as they want.

1 Corinthians 6:12
...People should never touch the stuff.
...People should be able to use alcohol, but not in excess.
...People have the right to use alcohol as much as they want.

Ephesians 5:18
...People should never touch the stuff.
...People should be able to use alcohol, but not in excess.
...People have the right to use alcohol as much as they want.

Colossians 3:17
...People should never touch the stuff.
...People should be able to use alcohol, but not in excess.
...People have the right to use alcohol as much as they want.

1 Peter 4:7
...People should never touch the stuff.
...People should be able to use alcohol, but not in excess.
...People have the right to use alcohol as much as they want.

# TEAM EFFORT

## THE BALLOON TRIBE[1]

There is a primitive tribe with a unique social activity. This is the story of how that activity originated and the effects it had on the tribe.

It seems that a short while back, one of the tribe members discovered a stretchy substance which came from a local tree. At first, the tribe didn't think this discovery was very important. However, from that substance one tribe member was able to invent what we know as a balloon. The tribe thought it a clever but seemingly useless invention.

One day, however, that same tribe member discovered something interesting about the balloons. After blowing up several of them, he became light-headed and out of breath, experiencing a euphoric, dizzy feeling. When he told this to the rest of the tribe, everyone immediately wanted to try it. Eventually, as this activity increased, the tribe became divided into four groups: The Dizzy Balloon Blowers, the Occasional Balloon Blowers, the Balloon Blowers for Career or Craft, and the Anti-Balloon Blowers.

The Dizzy Balloon Blowers developed a tolerance for blowing up several very large balloons in a short time—usually in just one evening. This group would get together every week and blow up numerous balloons for many different reasons. Some would do it to get dizzier than the time before; some as just a reason to get together with their friends; some because it was a way to relax after a hard day in the jungle; some to celebrate; and some because they weren't getting along with other tribe members. Each tribe member felt that his or her reason for blowing up balloons was worth it, though they often felt sick and nauseated in the morning.

Now the Occasional Balloon Blowers enjoyed a balloon every once in a while. In fact, when they did join the Dizzy group, they would take up a whole evening blowing up just one balloon (which was usually not too large). These tribe members blew up balloons for all the same reasons as the Dizzy group, but were careful to avoid having to go through what the Dizzies went through the morning after.

The Balloon Blowers for Career or Craft turned balloon blowing into an art. They only blew up the best balloons, not just any old cheap balloon. In fact, many of this group made their own balloons. And fine balloons they were! It was not long after balloons were discovered that this group started contests and competitions to find the best balloon. They examined balloon shape, size, color, and how well it expanded. Many in this group got very good at making balloons and did so full-time.

On the other side of the jungle were the Anti-Balloon Blowers. They had seen the effects from blowing up too many balloons and getting dizzy. They loudly protested that absolutely no one should blow up balloons! The Anti-Balloon Blowers said balloon blowing had caused tribe families to break up and hate one another. They argued that many tribe members had given up their tribal responsibilities so they could blow up balloons all day and get dizzy.

With the many groups of balloon blowers and the Anti-Balloon Blowers, it was difficult to assess the overall benefit or detriment to the tribe of the balloon blowing. Some members would not touch balloons while some seemingly could not face life without them. In some way every tribe member had to make up his or her own mind.

Group One: Blowing up balloons is fine, and it's okay to run out of breath and get dizzy if you feel like it.
Group Two: Occasional balloon blowing is okay, but it's morally wrong to get dizzy.
Group Three: Blowing up balloons is wrong at all times.

**Note**

1. Larry A. Dunn, *Ideas Number Thirty-seven* (Grand Rapids, MI: Zondervan, Youth Specialties, 1985), p. 30-31. Used by permission.

## TEAM EFFORT

### "JUST SAY NO" GAME

Role-play your situation from one of three positions: using drugs and alcohol is always okay, using drugs and alcohol is occasionally okay or using drugs and alcohol is always wrong.

**Alcohol Offers:**

1. Your sister and her friend pick you up from a party, and her friend offers you a cold beer for the trip home.

2. At a party, the gang gets into the parents' liquor cabinet. Everyone starts drinking out of a bottle of vodka.

3. Your parents take you out to a nice dinner at a local club. Your dad orders everyone something to drink and tells you it's okay for you to have one.

4. On a fishing trip, you go up the river with your brother. You are in the middle of the forest, and he says that since no one is around you can have a beer.

**Drug Offers:**

1. You are at school, between classes, and someone asks you to walk into the bathroom to smoke a joint.

2. A boy you know says he snuck some of his mother's tranquilizers out of the medicine cabinet. He asks you to meet him after school to take them.

3. One of the high school seniors offers to give you a ride home and tells you he has some crack that is pure and expensive.

4. At one of the local hangouts, a friend says she has some bottles of cough syrup. If you drink it, she promises you will feel as though you are in another world.

**THE FIGHT FOR CONTROL**

# IN THE WORD

## WHO'S IN CONTROL?

Read the following Scriptures. Check the position that is supported by each Scripture.

**Romans 8:5-8**

......People should never touch the stuff.

......People should be able to use alcohol, but not in excess.

......People have the right to use alcohol as much as they want.

**1 Corinthians 6:12**

......People should never touch the stuff.

......People should be able to use alcohol, but not in excess.

People have the right to use alcohol as much as they want.

**Ephesians 5:18**

......People should never touch the stuff.

......People should be able to use alcohol, but not in excess.

......People have the right to use alcohol as much as they want.

**Colossians 3:17**

......People should never touch the stuff.

......People should be able to use alcohol, but not in excess.

......People have the right to use alcohol as much as they want.

**1 Peter 4:7**

......People should never touch the stuff.

......People should be able to use alcohol, but not in excess.

......People have the right to use alcohol as much as they want.

**2 Peter 1:5-9**

......People should never touch the stuff.

......People should be able to use drugs or alcohol, but not in excess.

......People have the right to use alcohol as much as they want.

**1.** Do you think a person can be controlled by the Holy Spirit and get drunk or high at the same time? Why or why not?

..................................................................................................

..................................................................................................

**2.** Do you think that most teenagers are able to control drinking and/or drugs? Why or why not?

..................................................................................................

..................................................................................................

**3.** How would a person know if he or she had passed the point of being in control?

..................................................................................................

..................................................................................................

# SO WHAT?

Write out your philosophy and guidelines for drug and alcohol use.

........................................

........................................

........................................

........................................

........................................

........................................

........................................

# THINGS TO THINK ABOUT

**1.** Is using drugs or drinking necessarily a "Christian" issue? Why or why not?

.............................................................................................................................

.............................................................................................................................

.............................................................................................................................

**2.** Should you attend a party where you know drugs and drinking will be prevalent? Why or why not?

.............................................................................................................................

.............................................................................................................................

.............................................................................................................................

**3.** Should a Christian drink socially? Where would you draw the line?

.............................................................................................................................

.............................................................................................................................

.............................................................................................................................

.............................................................................................................................

# PARENT PAGE

**1.** Read Ephesians 5:18. What does this verse mean to you?

........................................................................................................

........................................................................................................

**2.** Do you know anyone who has had negative experiences with drugs and/or alcohol? How has this affected your own thoughts about the use of drugs or alcohol?

........................................................................................................

........................................................................................................

**3.** What if you were at a party and your best friend was becoming drunk, what advice would you give to him or her?

........................................................................................................

........................................................................................................

**4.** Do you agree or disagree with the following statement: Never put something in your body when you do not know how it will affect you? Give a reason for your answer.

........................................................................................................

........................................................................................................

**5.** Is it consistent for parents to have alcohol in their homes and forbid their children from drinking?

........................................................................................................

........................................................................................................

**6.** Here's what others say about alcohol:

"First the man takes a drink, then the drink takes a drink, then the drink takes a man..."—Japanese proverb

"The drunken man is a living corpse."—St. John Chrysostom

"O God, that men should put an enemy in their mouth to steal away their brains."—William Shakespeare

"Alcohol is a cancer in human society, eating out the vital and threatening destruction."—Abraham Lincoln

What's your personal philosophy on drug and alcohol use?

........................................................................................................

........................................................................................................

**Session 7 "The Fight for Control?"**
Date...........................
© 1994 by Gospel Light. Permission to photocopy granted.

# WHEN A FRIEND OR FAMILY MEMBER
# ABUSES DRUGS OR ALCOHOL

## **K**EY VERSE

"'Which of these three do you think was a neighbor to the man who fell into the hands of robbers?' The expert in the law replied, 'The one who had mercy on him.' Jesus told him, 'Go and do likewise.'"
Luke 10:36,37

## **B**IBLICAL BASIS

John 3:16; Luke 10:30-37

## **T**HE BIG IDEA

When a friend or family member has a potential drug or alcohol problem it affects more than one person. You can make some important decisions even if your friend or family member chooses not to change.

## **A**IMS OF THIS SESSION

During this session you will guide students to:
- Examine the family and common circumstances of an alcoholic or drug addict;
- Discover how God desires them to treat people in need;
- Commit to wise action in helping those with a drug or alcohol problem or a family member of a person with a drug or alcohol problem.

## **W**ARM UP

**Up a Tree—**
Teens identify with one of the people pictured.

## **T**EAM EFFORT— JUNIOR HIGH/ MIDDLE SCHOOL

**The Family Sculpture—**
A human sculpture of the family of an alcoholic or drug addict.

## **T**EAM EFFORT— HIGH SCHOOL

**Situation Role Plays—**
An opportunity for students to enact a substance abuse situation.

## **I**N THE WORD

**Good Samaritan Melodrama—**
A Bible study and melodrama on helping those in need.

## **T**HINGS TO THINK ABOUT (OPTIONAL)

Questions to get teens thinking and talking about helping those who abuse drugs and alcohol.

## **P**ARENT PAGE

A tool to get the session into the home and allow parents and teens to discuss the family of an alcoholic or drug addict.

## LEADER'S DEVOTIONAL

A cartoon recently made the rounds that showed a large convention hall. A banner was hung across the front, reading: WELCOME CHILDREN OF NORMAL PARENTS. Seated in the vast hall was an audience of three people!

Now, you may have had truly normal parents. But many have felt at one time or another that their upbringing *wasn't* normal. The term "dysfunctional" has become a buzz word. However, it's often used to excuse someone's problems instead of bringing an understanding of solutions. The example of having an elephant in your living room is an effective place to begin.

As you read through this lesson, stop to ask yourself: "What was the elephant in my parents' living room? What's the elephant in *my* living room?" It may not be substance abuse but something more common, such as addiction to anger or manipulation of others through guilt. An honest consideration of these questions may not make you comfortable! It can be a humbling experience. But only until you're ready to go on your own elephant hunt can you fully appreciate what a humbling effort it may take for one in your group who needs to help his or her own family or close friends.

The goal here is not to turn the class into a group therapy session or to turn your young people into a bunch of amateur psychologists. But don't be afraid of a show of emotions. Make it your goal to help your students understand that we are all sinners. We are all dysfunctional! The most important thing they can learn by understanding the problems of dysfunctional people (that's all of us) is that God is always bigger than any problem we can concoct, than any family style that has crippled us. As they learn to define problems, teach them to bring the problems before the Lord. Help them understand that as they pray earnestly, listen to God and obey Him, they can be part of His big plan to help someone else come into freedom from *whatever* addiction is holding him or her. (Mary Gross, editor, Gospel Light.)

**"If you want me back, you've got to clean yourself up."—**

Sixteen-year-old-girl addressing her crack-addicted mother, *Newsweek*, February 14, 1994

SESSION EIGHT

BIBLE TUCK-IN™

# WHEN A FRIEND OR FAMILY MEMBER
# ABUSES DRUGS OR ALCOHOL

## Key Verse

"Which of these three do you think was a neighbor to the man who fell into the hands of robbers?' The expert in the law replied, 'The one who had mercy on him.' Jesus told him, 'Go and do likewise.'" Luke 10:36,37

## Biblical Basis

John 3:16; Luke 10:30-37

## The Big Idea

When a friend or family member has a potential drug or alcohol problem it affects more than one person. You can make some important decisions even if your friend or family member chooses not to change.

## Warm Up (5-7 Minutes)

### Up a Tree

- Display a copy of "Up a Tree" on page 123 using an overhead projector.
- As a whole group, answer the questions. Allow students to pass on the question, "Why?"

Which person in this picture describes how you are feeling about yourself? Why?

---------------------------------------- Fold ----------------------------------------

## So What?

What can you do to help a person with a drug or alcohol problem? What can you do to help a family member of a person with a drug or alcohol problem? Keep in mind there is nothing you can do to change a person who abuses drugs or alcohol. You aren't responsible or the cause of the behavior.

Consider contacting local organizations that specialize in the treatment of alcoholism and drug abuse and those that help the loved ones of abusers (A.A., Alateen, etc.).

## Things to Think About (Optional)

- Use the questions on page 129 after or as a part of "In the Word."
1. If a friend drinks and doesn't want to quit which philosophy is the best idea?
   a. Back off the friendship.
   b. Confront the issues.
   c. It's his or her life, as long as it doesn't affect me.
   d. Preach at him or her.
   e. Encourage him or her to get some help.
   f. Other _____

2. Do you agree or disagree with the following statement: People with drinking or drug problems sometimes don't need our help? Give a reason for your answer.

..............................................................................

3. What do you think causes a person to abuse drugs or alcohol?

..............................................................................

## Parent Page

- Distribute page to parents.

## THE FAMILY SCULPTURE

- Build the family sculpture, which demonstrates the roles various family members assume.

- As you help students assume various parts, explain why each person is placed as he or she is.

1. Addict (Father)—Stand him on a chair in the front. He is the focus of family, the key figure.

2. Enabler (Mother)—Stand her next to the father. He leans on her, putting some of his weight on her so she feels the pressure of his addiction. She may get upset and throw away his drugs or alcohol, but she will continue to enable him.

3. Hero (Child)—He/she helps Mother support Father. He/she has one arm on both parents. Hero does it all: takes care of Mother and Father, is active in church youth group, works a job to help, gets all As. Hero wants Father to be proud. Mother calls on him/her for support.

4. Lost Child (Child)—He/she stands with his/her face against the wall. Lost Child withdraws from the family. Much of the family conversation is about his/her attitude and actions. Lost Child leaves the home early and spends little time in communication with family.

5. The Clown (Child)—He/she walks around the family and tickles them. The Clown hurts like everyone else but deals with the hurt by laughing it off.

6. Scapegoat (Child)—He/she walks around the family and karate chops everyone. Scapegoat takes the focus off Father. He/she often gets attention by copying Father's behavior by using drugs or alcohol.

- As a whole group, discuss the following questions.

1. How did it feel to portray Father? Mother? Hero? Lost Child? etc.

2. Do you think this is an accurate portrayal of the family of an alcoholic or drug addict? Why or why not?

- - - - - - - - - - - - - - - - Fold - - - - - - - - - - - - - -

## SITUATION ROLE PLAYS

- Divide students into groups of three or four.

- Display a copy of "Situation Role Plays" on page 123 using an overhead projector.

- Students choose a role play to perform.

- As a whole group, discuss role plays.

**Here are two role plays to act out and then discuss.**

1. **You confront your best friend about the fact that he or she has been partying way too much. The friend is defensive and doesn't want to admit a problem.**

2. **Dad is an alcoholic. Mom and the three children sit down to discuss Dad's problem. They come up with a plan to confront Dad. Now bring Dad into the picture and actually have the confrontation. Dad is defensive and starts blaming his problems on them.**

## IN THE WORD (25-33 MINUTES)

### GOOD SAMARITAN MELODRAMA

- Assign the melodrama roles.

- Give the Narrator a copy of "Good Samaritan Melodrama" on pages 125.

- As Narrator reads melodrama, characters perform actions.

- Give each student a copy of "Good Samaritan Melodrama" and a pen or pencil.

- As a whole group, complete the Bible study.

1. **Read the real account in Luke 10:30-37. Describe the different styles of help offered by the:**

**Priest**

**Levite**

**Samaritan**

2. **What does the Samaritan teach us about helping a person in need?**

# WARM UP

### UP A TREE

Which person in this picture describes how you are feeling about yourself? Why?

...............................................................................................................

...............................................................................................................

...............................................................................................................

...............................................................................................................

...............................................................................................................

# TEAM EFFORT

### SITUATION ROLE PLAYS

Here are two role plays to act out and then discuss.

**1.** You confront your best friend about the fact that he or she has been partying way too much. The friend is defensive and doesn't want to admit a problem.

**2.** Dad is an alcoholic. Mom and the three children sit down to discuss Dad's problem. They come up with a plan to confront Dad. Now bring Dad into the picture and actually have the confrontation. Dad is defensive and starts blaming his problems on them.

# IN THE WORD

## GOOD SAMARITAN MELODRAMA

Characters:

**Narrator    Levite    Man    Samaritan    Drug Dealers    Donkey    Priest**

Once upon a time a young man minding his own business and whistling a merry tune (whistle) was walking to a distant land. When all of a sudden three of the ugliest drug dealers attacked him, robbed him and kicked him while he was down. The young man lay on the ground moaning and groaning, whining and whimpering.

A priest came along the road singing "Amazing Grace" and carrying his Bible. He/she walked up to the man and said, "Son, you should be ashamed of yourself. You are a disgrace to the church. Please leave this area at once." And the priest walked on singing "Amazing Grace."

Next came a Levite wearing Levis. He/she was also a religious person and was carrying 10 Bibles. The Levite stopped to see the man in need and quickly said, "I have a verse for you." The Levite read John 3:16 and said, "That should do for a scum like you."

Finally, along came a Samaritan riding on a donkey and singing:

> A good Samaritan rode his donkey,
> far away from home.
> Saw a man beside the road,
> and fixed a broken bone.
> (Sung to the tune of "Yankee Doodle.")

He/she then got off the donkey and bandaged up the man. The Samaritan gave him some water and put him across the donkey to take him for help and shelter.

**1.** Read the real account in Luke 10:30-37. Describe the different styles of help offered by the:

Priest.........................................................................................................
.........................................................................................................
.........................................................................................................

Levite.........................................................................................................
.........................................................................................................
.........................................................................................................

Samaritan.........................................................................................................
.........................................................................................................

**2.** What does the Samaritan teach us about helping a person in need?

.........................................................................................................
.........................................................................................................
.........................................................................................................
.........................................................................................................

**125**

# So WHAT?

Keep in mind there is nothing you can do to change a person who abuses drugs or alcohol. You aren't responsible or the cause of the behavior. What can you do to help a person with a drug or alcohol problem? What can you do to help a family member of a person with a drug or alcohol problem?

...................................................................................................................................

...................................................................................................................................

...................................................................................................................................

...................................................................................................................................

...................................................................................................................................

Consider contacting local organizations that specialize in the treatment of alcoholism and drug abuse and those that help the loved ones of abusers (A.A., Alateen, etc.).

# Things to Think About

**1.** If a friend drinks and doesn't want to quit which philosophy is the best idea:

a. Back off the friendship.

b. Confront the issues.

c. It's his or her life, as long as it doesn't affect me.

d. Preach at him or her.

e. Encourage him or her to get some help.

f. Other.........................................................................

**2.** Do you agree or disagree with the following statement: People with drinking or drug problems sometimes don't need our help? Give a reason for your answer.

.................................................................................................

.................................................................................................

.................................................................................................

**3.** What do you think causes a person to abuse drugs or alcohol?

.................................................................................................

.................................................................................................

.................................................................................................

.................................................................................................

# PARENT PAGE

## THE ELEPHANT IN THE LIVING ROOM

An elephant is in the living room. Living with an alcoholic or drug addict is often compared to living with an elephant in your living room. The family washes and feeds the elephant. They clean up its messes, but seldom do they discuss the real problem of having an elephant in the living room. Sometimes they erupt with anger over the elephant, but most of the time they act as if it is fairly normal to have an elephant in the living room.

**1. What do you think of this illustration?**

..............................................................................................................................

..............................................................................................................................

..............................................................................................................................

**2. Does our family have any elephants in the living room?**

..............................................................................................................................

..............................................................................................................................

..............................................................................................................................

**3. If yes, what is it and what can we do about it? After discussing the issue(s), list suggestions of what you can do. Now take a few minutes to pray together about these issues.**

..............................................................................................................................

..............................................................................................................................

..............................................................................................................................

**4. If no, take a few minutes as a family to offer a prayer of thanksgiving for each family member.**

..............................................................................................................................

..............................................................................................................................

..............................................................................................................................

**Session 8 "When a Friend or Family Member Abuses Drugs or Alcohol"**
**Date**..............................

## Unit III

# ROCK 'N' ROLL

## LEADER'S PEP TALK

### WHO'S INFLUENCING YOUR TEENS?

Today's young people live in a media-bombarded generation. If it's not music then it's movies. If it's not movies then it's magazines. If it's not magazines then it's the good ole TV. Mix them all and it's MTV.

The average teenager watches 10 hours a week of MTV, compared to spending 1.4 hours a week at church. Robert Pittman, former president and chief executive director of MTV, said, "Early on, we made a key decision that we would be the voice of young America. We were building more than just a channel. We were building a culture."

Rock expert Al Menconi believes that rock music meets three of youth's basic needs:

1. The rock star (via tapes, compact discs and videos) spends huge amounts of time with the young people—providing companionship.

2. The rock star accepts the young person as they are—providing acceptance.

3. The rock star relates to the young person's problems—providing identification.

Fulfilling the need of companionship, acceptance and identification is all a part of youth ministry. Is it possible that the secular rock culture has done a better job in these areas than many parents and youth workers?

At times, I've been criticized for talking about rock music from some who say, "Stick to the Bible." We need to help our young generation "learn to discern" what kind of "stuff" they are putting in their minds and how it subtly, or not so subtly, affects them. And the way we'll do that is through the Word.

Paul gave some great advice when he wrote:

> Finally, brothers, whatever is true, whatever is noble, whatever is right, whatever is pure, whatever is lovely, whatever is admirable—if anything is excellent or praiseworthy—think about such things. Whatever you have learned or received or heard from me, or seen in me—put it into practice. And the God of peace will be with you (Philippians 4:8,9).

**133**

Our job in these four sessions is to help teens see the powerful influence of music and the media on their lives and to develop a Christian approach to their listening and viewing habits.

**Let's not underestimate the facts that:**

1. Rock music is here to stay.
2. Most students listen each day to several hours of secular music.
3. Music and the media does influence our teens to a greater extent than we realize.
4. Many of the "heroes" of rock music have lifestyles and philosophies that are opposed to God.
5. Most students have not really thought from a Christian viewpoint about the music and media that are influencing their lives.
6. Young people will listen to you and are interested in 'how music does or does not influence them spiritually as long as the presentation is done with grace and understanding.

With these points in mind, I personally hope you have great sessions on one of your young people's most influential and, perhaps, most controversial subjects. You're making a difference by bringing up issues like this. God bless you!

# ROCK REALITY

## **K**EY VERSE

"**D**o not love the world or anything in the world. If anyone loves the world, the love of the Father is not in him." 1 John 2:15

## **B**IBLICAL BASIS

**J**ames 4:4-8;
**1** Peter 2:9-12;
**1** John 2:15-17; 4:1-5

## **T**HE BIG IDEA

**T**eens need to develop biblical principles for listening to secular music (rock, rap, alternative, country, etc.).

## **A**IMS OF THIS SESSION

**D**uring this session you will guide students to:

- Examine the message of most secular music;
- Discover the contrast between the message of most secular music and God's message;
- Develop guidelines for listening or not listening to secular music.

## **W**ARM UP

**Rock Favorites—**
Students share their music favorites.

## **T**EAM EFFORT— JUNIOR HIGH/ MIDDLE SCHOOL

**To Take a Stand—**
An agree/disagree activity on secular music.

## **T**EAM EFFORT— HIGH SCHOOL

**Lyrics or Leerics?—**
An evaluation of the message of secular music.

## **I**N THE WORD

**On the Air—**
A Bible study on "not loving the world" and setting music-listening guidelines.

## **T**HINGS TO THINK ABOUT (OPTIONAL)

**Q**uestions to get teens thinking and talking about secular music.

## **P**ARENT PAGE

**A** tool to get the session into the home and allow parents and teens to discuss their music-listening standards.

## LEADER'S DEVOTIONAL

During the Renaissance, printed copies of popular music were published for the first time. Sheets called "broadsides" passed from hand to hand. Before the advent of printing, live performance circulated popular music from one person to the next. But in the past hundred years, circulation has speeded up considerably, due to inventions from the gramophone to MTV. In whatever form it's passed around, every generation can probably point to a song or two that has been "theirs," setting that generation apart from others.

As a generation grows up, it seeks to be identified, to be different from the last generation. Pastimes, fashions and music are the most visible ways we older folks notice this.

Until the dissolution of society as we know it, popular music is not going to go away. The classics aren't going to suddenly take over that spot marked for popular music in every teen's heart. As Neil Young has sung so often, "Rock and roll will never die." A lot of young people are banking on that for their identification.

The trouble is, of course, that song lyrics send messages. And they are often messages that we'd rather our students did not hear and espouse. The world's philosophies about life's most important issues—love, respect, honesty and so forth—are often dead wrong. Set to music, these philosophies become singable lyrics, repeatable and, therefore, even more memorable. It's not so much that we're afraid our teens will take some rocker's admonition to kill their parents or commit suicide; our teens can spot those messages. The twisted philosophies in songs are much more subtle than that. However, they can be just as destructive.

We've talked earlier about the fact that Satan loves to destroy relationships. Help your young people to focus on the ways relationships are dealt with by popular music, whether rap, hip-hop, country western or rock 'n' roll. Help your students understand that even while they identify with their generation, they are also members of another generation—God's chosen generation. They don't have to believe everything they hear. (Mary Gross, editor, Gospel Light.)

**"They're expecting someone who's treading water to save them....I can barely keep myself together."—**

Eddie Veder,
musician, *Musician*,
November 1993

# ROCK REALITY

## K EY VERSE

"Do not love the world or anything in the world. If anyone loves the world, the love of the Father is not in him." 1 John 2:15

## B IBLICAL BASIS

James 4:4-8; 1 Peter 2:9-12; 1 John 2:15-17; 4:1-5

## T HE BIG IDEA

Teens need to develop biblical principles for listening to secular music (rock, rap, alternative, country, etc.).

## W ARM UP (5-7 MINUTES)

### ROCK FAVORITES

• As a whole group, answer the following questions. Go around the group having each student answer the first question. Repeat with the second and third questions.

What's your favorite kind of music?

What's your favorite radio station?

Who is your favorite musician or group?

---- Fold ----

## T HINGS TO THINK ABOUT (OPTIONAL)

• Use the questions on page 143 after or as a part of "In the Word."

1. How big a part in your life does secular music play? How many hours a day do you listen to it?

2. What do you think Jesus would say about secular music?

3. Were our parents as influenced by secular music as our generation? Explain.

## P ARENT PAGE

• Distribute page to parents.

# TEAM EFFORT—JUNIOR HIGH/MIDDLE SCHOOL (15-20 MINUTES)

## TO TAKE A STAND

- Create a "Strongly Agree" sign, an "Agree" sign, an "Undecided" sign, a "Disagree" sign and a "Strongly Disagree" sign. Place the five signs at different locations throughout the room.
- Read aloud each of the following statements.
- After each statement is read, students move to the sign that most clearly represents what they believe.
- Students report why they voted the way they did.

The majority of secular musicians are moral people.

Contemporary Christian music is as good as secular music.

Secular music can be harmful.

It's okay to listen to secular music as long as you don't listen to the lyrics.

It is impossible to be a strong Christian and listen to secular music.

# TEAM EFFORT—HIGH SCHOOL (15-20 MINUTES)

## LYRICS OR LEERICS?

- Play or show several popular songs or videos. (You may ask students to bring some. Make sure you preview them before use.)
- Give each student a copy of "Lyrics or Leerics?" on page 139 and a pen or pencil.
- As a whole group, choose 10 songs or videos to evaluate.
- Students complete the chart.

**After listing 10 popular song or video titles in the left-hand column, place a check mark under each of the themes in the right-hand columns that applies to the songs or videos you selected.**

### THEMES

| Song/Video Title | | Song/Video Title | |
|---|---|---|---|
| Alcohol/Drugs | | Hedonism (Party on!) | |
| Anarchy | | Materialism | |
| Anger/Aggression | | Occult/Satanism | |
| Anti-Authority | | People as Objects | |
| Anti-God | | Permissive Sex | |
| Crude Language | | Perverted Sex | |
| Escape | | Prejudice Rebellion | |
| Death | | Self-Abuse | |
| Gloom & Doom/Despair | | Violence/Destruction | |

Fold

# ON THE WORD (25-33 MINUTES)

## ON THE AIR

- Give each student a copy of "On the Air" on page 141 and a pen or pencil.
- Students individually complete the Bible study.
- As a whole group, discuss the questions.

**As music director at the local radio station, you are responsible for choosing the songs to be played on your station.**

**1. Read the following Scriptures. What programming guidelines would they help you establish?**

**James 4:4-8**
(The world and God are at odds. If you choose the world's message, you're at odds with God.)

**1 Peter 2:9-12**
(We are to be separate from the world and its way of life. Abstain from any evil.)

**1 John 2:15-17**
(We are not to love the world and its standards. They will pass away.)

**1 John 4:1-5**
(If people do not acknowledge Jesus, they are not of God. If they are from the world, they'll deliver a worldly message.)

**2. What musicians or groups would you definitely not air?**

**3. What musicians or groups would you definitely air?**

# SO WHAT?

**Do these guidelines fit with your music-listening habits? How will you change your habits?**

# TEAM EFFORT

### LYRICS OR LEERICS?[1]

After listing 10 popular song or video titles in the left-hand column, place a check mark under each of the themes in the right-hand columns that applies to the songs or videos you selected.

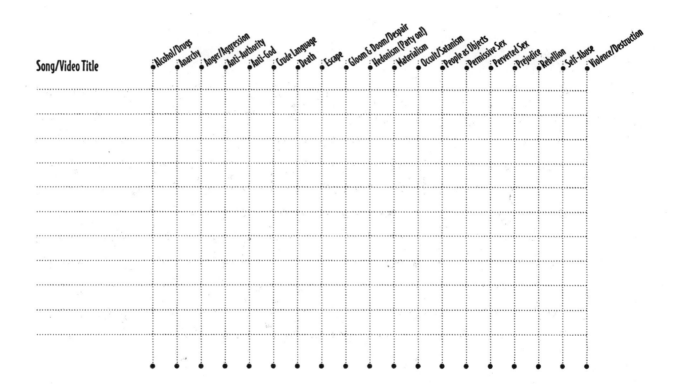

| Song/Video Title | Alcohol/Drugs | Anarchy | Anger/Aggression | Anti-Authority | Anti-God | Crude Language | Death | Escape | Gloom & Doom/Despair | Hedonism (Party on!) | Materialism | Occult/Satanism | People as Objects | Permissive Sex | Perverted Sex | Prejudice | Rebellion | Self-Abuse | Violence/Destruction |
|---|---|---|---|---|---|---|---|---|---|---|---|---|---|---|---|---|---|---|---|
| | | | | | | | | | | | | | | | | | | | |

**Note**

1. David Lynn, *Rock Talk* (Grand Rapids, MI: Zondervan, Youth Specialties, 1991), p. 31. Used by permission.

# IN THE WORD

## ON THE AIR

As music director at the local radio station, you are responsible for choosing the songs to be played on your station.

**1. Read the following Scriptures. What programming guidelines would they help you establish?**

James 4:4-8

.........................................................................................................................

.........................................................................................................................

1 Peter 2:9-12

.........................................................................................................................

.........................................................................................................................

1 John 2:15-17

.........................................................................................................................

.........................................................................................................................

1 John 4:1-5

.........................................................................................................................

.........................................................................................................................

**2. What musicians or groups would you definitely not air?**

.........................................................................................................................

.........................................................................................................................

.........................................................................................................................

**3. What musicians or groups would you definitely air?**

.........................................................................................................................

.........................................................................................................................

.........................................................................................................................

.........................................................................................................................

# SO WHAT?

Do these guidelines fit with your music listening habits? How will you change your habits?

.........................................................................................................................

.........................................................................................................................

.........................................................................................................................

.........................................................................................................................

.........................................................................................................................

141

# THINGS TO THINK ABOUT

**1.** How big a part in your life does secular music play? How many hours a day do you listen to it?

.........................................................................................................................

.........................................................................................................................

.........................................................................................................................

.........................................................................................................................

**2.** What do you think Jesus would say about secular music?

.........................................................................................................................

.........................................................................................................................

.........................................................................................................................

.........................................................................................................................

**3.** Were our parents as influenced by secular music as our generation? Explain.

.........................................................................................................................

.........................................................................................................................

.........................................................................................................................

# Parent Page

## For Parent

**1. As a teen, who were your favorite musicians and groups?**

.........................................................................................................................................................................

.........................................................................................................................................................................

.........................................................................................................................................................................

**2. What were some of your favorite songs?**

.........................................................................................................................................................................

.........................................................................................................................................................................

.........................................................................................................................................................................

**3. Do you think secular music has changed over the years? Explain.**

.........................................................................................................................................................................

.........................................................................................................................................................................

.........................................................................................................................................................................

**4. What did your parents say about your listening to secular music?**

.........................................................................................................................................................................

.........................................................................................................................................................................

.........................................................................................................................................................................

## The Music Agreement

Together come up with a reasonable agreement about music in the home.

Hours music can be on in the home .........................................................................................................

Any groups or music not allowed in the home ...............................................................................

Concerts I could or could not attend ...............................................................................................

**Session I "Rock Reality" Date**............................

# GIGO (GARBAGE IN/ GARBAGE OUT)

##  KEY VERSE

"Finally, brothers, whatever is true, whatever is noble, whatever is right, whatever is pure, whatever is lovely, whatever is admirable—if anything is excellent or praiseworthy—think about such things." Philippians 4:8

## BIBLICAL BASIS

Proverbs 13:20; 14:7;
Romans 12:2;
Philippians 4:8;
Colossians 3:1-4;
Hebrews 12:1-3

## THE BIG IDEA

Whatever young people put into their minds will eventually come out. Put garbage in, garbage comes out.

##  AIMS OF THIS SESSION

During this session you will guide students to:

- Examine the influence music has on their minds and actions;
- Discover how they can use their minds to help them live more Christian lifestyles;
- Pray for an awareness of negative influences and God's protection over their minds.

## WARM UP

**Checking In—**
An opportunity for teens to share.

## TEAM EFFORT— JUNIOR HIGH/ MIDDLE SCHOOL

**The Great Debate—**
A look at the the pros and cons of secular music.

## TEAM EFFORT— HIGH SCHOOL

**Musical Influences—**
An agree/disagree activity on the influence of secular music.

## IN THE WORD

**Your Mind Matters—**
A Bible study on focusing our minds on what matters.

## THINGS TO THINK ABOUT (OPTIONAL)

Questions to get teens thinking and talking about secular music.

## PARENT PAGE

A tool to get the session into the home and allow parents and teens to discuss secular music and musicians.

## Leader's Devotional

Let's talk about the power of music for a minute. Think back to the days when you were a teen. Which popular songs do you still remember the lyrics to? (Some of us would have to confess to knowing more lyrics than Bible verses!) What songs had a kind of power in your life or changed your mind about something?

Music springs from the heart. And because of this, it involves us emotionally as we identify with the feelings of the writer or singer. Then we acknowledge or reject the content of the lyrics. But the desire to identify with the singer/lyricist can be so strong that even though conscience can't agree to the content of the lyrics as true or good, well, we just sing along anyway. And that active participation in the song reinforces the false ideas in the mind.

Those lyric phrases seem so neat, so adult, so well turned when you're a young person groping to understand love and relationships, truth and justice. "Don't get mad, get even...love the one you're with...only the good die young..." The list is endless and the truths are few. But those errors in thinking are often very nicely put. In fact, Satan must have a whole poetry division working overtime!

Music is far too powerful to be treated as casually as we do. It's never value-neutral because it's a cry of the heart. The question is, whose heart is doing the crying out? Whose heart will we follow? Help your students to practice using the "filter test" given by God in Philippians 4:8. After they've practiced this in class, encourage them to try using the test just for a week—at home, in the car, with friends. Encourage them to rewrite the lyrics of songs for themselves, to actually reflect and clarify what they do believe. And let them know it's okay to write their own lyrics! If God has put new songs in their hearts, they don't have to sing along with the lies of the world any longer. (Mary Gross, editor, Gospel Light.)

**"Wearing a dress shows I can be as feminine as I want. I'm a heterosexual...big deal. But if I were a homosexual, it wouldn't matter either."—**

Kurt Cobain, musician,
*L.A. Times Calendar*,
August 29, 1993

# GIGO (GARBAGE IN/ GARBAGE OUT)

## Key Verse

"Finally, brothers, whatever is true, whatever is noble, whatever is right, whatever is pure, whatever is lovely, whatever is admirable—if anything is excellent or praiseworthy—think about such things." Philippians 4:8

## Biblical Basis

Proverbs 13:20; 14:7; Romans 12:2; Philippians 4:8; Colossians 3:1-4; Hebrews 12:1-3

## The Big Idea

Whatever young people put into their minds will eventually come out. Put garbage in, garbage comes out.

## Warm Up (5-7 Minutes)

### Checking In

- Display a copy or "Checking In" on page 151 using an overhead projector.
- Divide students into groups of three or four.
- Students discuss questions.

What was the high point of your week?
Describe one goal you completed this week.
What did you put off this week?
Did you make any plans this week for future happenings?

---------- Fold ----------

**149**

## Parent Page

- Distribute page to parents.

## THE GREAT DEBATE

• Divide students into two groups. If the two groups are too large, divide them into four or six groups.
• Assign one group to be pro-secular music and one group to be anti-secular music.
• Students defend their positions to the whole group.

## TEAM EFFORT—HIGH SCHOOL (15-20 Minutes)

### MUSICAL INFLUENCES

• Read aloud the following statements.
• If a student agrees with the statement, he or she should stand on the right side of the room. If a student disagrees, he or she should stand on the left side of the room.
• Students give reasons for their responses.

1. Secular music can have a positive effect on our lives.
2. Listening to secular music can create poor relationships with family and friends.
3. Some of the negative words in certain songs can infiltrate your mind.
4. Secular music can fool your emotions.
5. Some secular musicians or groups have very negative lifestyles.
6. Some secular music lyrics have an important message for our generation.
7. Some secular musicians or groups are definitely anti-God in words and lifestyle.
8. Most people are not aware of the influence that secular music has on people's lives.

## IN THE WORD (25-33 Minutes)

### YOUR MIND MATTERS

• Divide students into groups of three or four.
• Give each student a copy of "Your Mind Matters" on page 151 and a pen or pencil.
• Students complete the Bible study.

1. Keep away from negative influences. Read Proverbs 13:20 and 14:7.
a. What are common negative influences?

(Negative influences can be the media, peers and well-known people.)

Fold

b. Why are people drawn to negative influences even when they know they are bad for them?

(There is something very attractive and enticing about many evil desires.)

2. Constantly renew your mind. Read Romans 12:2 and Colossians 3:1-4.
a. How can we be constantly renewing our minds?

(Our minds are renewed by filling them with God's truth, His Word.)

b. What does it mean to "set your minds on things above"?

(It means to dwell on holy things and think on a godly level.)

3. Think about good things. Read Philippians 4:8. For each phrase, list one way you can think on that quality (true, noble, right, etc.).

a. Whatever is true
b. Whatever is noble
c. Whatever is right
d. Whatever is pure
e. Whatever is lovely
f. Whatever is admirable
g. Whatever is excellent or praiseworthy

## SO WHAT?

How does the music you listen to compare with Philippians 4:8? Spend a few minutes in individual prayer for an awareness of negative influences in your life. Then as a group pray for God's protection over your minds.

## THINGS TO THINK ABOUT (OPTIONAL)

• Use the questions on page 153 after or as a part of "In the Word."

1. Of today's musicians or groups, who would you say has the most negative lyrics?

2. Do you think the beat of the music can have sexual or violent influences in a person's life? Why or why not?

3. What musicians or groups today are a positive influence on our minds and actions?

GIGO
(GARBAGE IN/
GARBAGE OUT)

# WARM UP

## CHECKING IN

What was the high point of your week?....................................................................

............................................................................................................................

Describe one goal you completed this week.............................................................

............................................................................................................................

What did you put off this week?..............................................................................

............................................................................................................................

Did you make any plans this week for future happenings?.........................................

............................................................................................................................

# IN THE WORD

## YOUR MIND MATTERS

**1.** Keep away from negative influences. Read Proverbs 13:20 and 14:7.
   a. What are common negative influences?.............................................................

............................................................................................................................

   b. Why are people drawn to negative influences even when they know they are bad for them?

............................................................................................................................

**2.** Constantly renew your mind. Read Romans 12:2 and Colossians 3:1-4.
   a. How can we be constantly renewing our minds?...............................................

............................................................................................................................

   b. What does it mean to "set your minds on things above"?...................................

............................................................................................................................

**3.** Think about good things. Read Philippians 4:8. For each phrase, list one way you can think on that quality (true, noble, right, etc.).
   a. Whatever is true...............................................................................................

............................................................................................................................

   b. Whatever is noble............................................................................................

............................................................................................................................

   c. Whatever is right ............................................................................................

   d. Whatever is pure..............................................................................................

............................................................................................................................

   e. Whatever is lovely............................................................................................

............................................................................................................................

   f. Whatever is admirable......................................................................................

............................................................................................................................

   g. Whatever is excellent or praiseworthy.............................................................

............................................................................................................................

# SO WHAT?

How does the music you listen to compare with Philippians 4:8? Spend a few minutes in individual prayer for an awareness of negative influences in your life. Then as a group pray for God's protection over your minds.

............................................................................................................................

............................................................................................................................

............................................................................................................................

## THINGS TO THINK ABOUT

**1.** Of today's musicians or groups, who would you say has the most negative lyrics?

.............................................................................................................................

.............................................................................................................................

.............................................................................................................................

**2.** Do you think the beat of the music can have sexual or violent influences in a person's life? Why or why not?

.............................................................................................................................

.............................................................................................................................

.............................................................................................................................

**3.** What musicians or groups today are a positive influence on our minds and actions?

.............................................................................................................................

.............................................................................................................................

.............................................................................................................................

.............................................................................................................................

# PARENT PAGE

## HEROES OR ??

Throughout the history of rock 'n' roll there have been many heroes and role models who might have been incredible musicians but who "crashed and burned" in their own personal lives. Read the list below from the parent's generation.

• Brian Jones (of the Rolling Stones), who died of a drug overdose, July 5, 1969.

• Jimi Hendrix, who died of a heroin overdose, September 18, 1970.

• Janis Joplin, who died of a heroin overdose, October 4, 1970.

• Jim Morrison, who died of a drug overdose, July 3, 1971.

**1.** What were the ingredients that caused these people to make such unwise lifestyle choices?

........................................................................................................

........................................................................................................

**2.** How did their lives influence others?

........................................................................................................

........................................................................................................

**3.** What must we do to not put our faith in humans who are fallible?

........................................................................................................

........................................................................................................

**4.** What do you think of this quote from Madonna: "The actors and singers and entertainers I know are emotional cripples. Really healthy people aren't in this business, let's face it."?[1]

........................................................................................................

........................................................................................................

## FOR THE TEEN

Give your parent a two-minute lesson on who the popular musicians of the day are and what possible negative behavior they might exhibit.

**1.** Why is it better to put our faith and trust in Christ?

........................................................................................................

........................................................................................................

**2.** Why is Hebrews 12:1-3 such good advice?

........................................................................................................

........................................................................................................

**Note**

1. Stephen Arterburn and Jim Burns, *When Love Is Not Enough* (Colorado Springs, CO: Focus on the Family, 1992), p. 53.

Session 10 "GIGO Garbage In/Garbage Out"

Date............................

# CONTEMPORARY CHRISTIAN MUSIC

## **K**EY VERSE

"Praise the Lord. Praise God in his sanctuary; praise him in his mighty heavens. Praise him for his acts of power; praise him for his surpassing greatness. Praise him with the sounding of the trumpet, praise him with the harp and lyre, praise him with tambourine and dancing, praise him with the strings and flute, praise him with the clash of cymbals, praise him with resounding cymbals. Let everything that has breath praise the Lord. Praise the Lord." Psalm 150

## **B**IBLICAL BASIS

Psalm 150

## **T**HE BIG IDEA

Contemporary Christian music is a positive alternative for teens.

## **A**IMS OF THIS SESSION

During this session you will guide students to:

- Examine the positive alternative of contemporary Christian music;
- Discover the many benefits of listening to music with a biblical message;
- Implement a decision to make positive, Christ-honoring music a part of their lives.

## **W**ARM UP

**Time Is on My Side—**
Students share what they like to do with their time.

## **T**EAM EFFORT— JUNIOR HIGH/ MIDDLE SCHOOL

**Sing a Song—**
Teens develop new lyrics for old tunes.

## **T**EAM EFFORT— HIGH SCHOOL

**Contemporary Christian Music Diet—**
A listing of popular contemporary Christian musicians.

## **I**N THE WORD

**Praise Him with the Synthesizer—**
A Bible study on music that praises God and a look at contemporary Christian music.

## **T**HINGS TO THINK ABOUT (OPTIONAL)

Questions to get teens thinking and talking about contemporary Christian music.

## **P**ARENT PAGE

A tool to get the session into the home and allow parents and teens to discuss contemporary Christian music.

## LEADER'S DEVOTIONAL

You might hum a song all day, to finally realize that it was the last thing you heard before you turned off the radio. God seems to have made our memories that way, for we seem to have a capacity for carrying a song around with us nearly all the time.

Of course, we believers are told in Colossians 3 that as Christ's word dwells in us, we will sing and make melody in our hearts to the Lord. It seems to be a spontaneous thing, tied to grateful hearts and minds that are dwelling on God. And judging by the flood of new music available that praises and honors the Lord, many people are sharing the songs of their hearts!

Now some may object to contemporary Christian music. It's okay to prefer hymns or cantatas or oratorios. But remember these were once contemporary Christian music, too. (For instance, the tune for the Thanksgiving hymn "We Gather Together" was originally a bar song about a girl named Matilda.) Tunes and song styles for songs of praise to God have often come from popular music simply because it was singable and familiar, the musical vernacular of that particular generation. We may not like every song style that comes down the pike but, as we've seen, it's lyric content that is the key element. And although we need to be discerning (some songs that purport to be Christian are weak in content), we can be thankful that there are a wealth of songs of many styles to which we can sing along with free hearts and clear consciences. There's no spiritual merit in one song style over another!

And just as we talked about the importance of every generation finding its own identification, so also must every generation of believers find their own songs with which to praise God, to make His truth their own. As we drop our prejudices and let our own hearts sing for joy to God, we will find the grace to plug some patience in our ears and let our students crank up the volume to praise God. If it's not our style, so much the better! (Mary Gross, editor, Gospel Light.)

**"When you take God and absolute morals out of society, then people will believe anything. And that's worse than believing nothing."—**

Wes King, Christian musician, Campus Life, July/August 1993

# CONTEMPORARY CHRISTIAN MUSIC

## KEY VERSE

"Praise the Lord. Praise God in his sanctuary; praise him in his mighty heavens. Praise him for his acts of power; praise him for his surpassing greatness. Praise him with the sounding of the trumpet, praise him with the harp and lyre, praise him with tambourine and dancing, praise him with the strings and flute, praise him with the clash of cymbals, praise him with resounding cymbals. Let everything that has breath praise the Lord. Praise the Lord." Psalm 150

## BIBLICAL BASIS

Psalm 150

## THE BIG IDEA

Contemporary Christian music is a positive alternative for teens.

## WARM UP (5-10 MINUTES)

### TIME IS ON MY SIDE

- Display a copy of "Time Is on My Side" on page 161 using an overhead projector.
- Students choose one statement to complete.
- Students who chose number one respond first. Students who chose number two respond second. Students who chose number three respond third.

1. When I have time to myself I like to...

2. When I have time with just one special friend I like to...

3. When I'm hanging out with the group I like to...

---
Fold
---

# TEAM EFFORT—JUNIOR HIGH/MIDDLE SCHOOL (15-20 MINUTES)

## SING A SONG

- Divide students into groups of three or four.
- Assign each group the tune of a well-known song ("Happy Birthday," a top 40 hit, "Mary Had a Little Lamb," etc.)
- Students write new lyrics about your youth group for the tune.
- Students share lyrics with whole group.

# TEAM EFFORT—HIGH SCHOOL (15-20 MINUTES)

## CONTEMPORARY CHRISTIAN MUSIC DIET

- Give each student a copy of "Contemporary Christian Music Diet" on page 161 and a pen or pencil.
- As a whole group, complete the list.

List your top five Christian musicians or groups and then fill in the information below.

**Top Five Christian Musicians**

| Name | Style of Music | Favorite Song |
|------|----------------|---------------|
| 1. | | |
| 2. | | |
| 3. | | |
| 4. | | |
| 5. | | |

# IN THE WORD (25-30 MINUTES)

## PRAISE HIM WITH THE SYNTHESIZER

- Invite a guest from a local Christian book store or a guest with a wide variety of contemporary Christian music to play CDs or tapes for this session.
- As a whole group, listen to samples of contemporary Christian music.
- Give each student a copy of "Praise Him with the Synthesizer" on page 163 and a pen or pencil.
- As a whole group, complete the Bible study.

---

Read Psalm 150. Now think about the world you live in (the different types of people, places, things, situations, etc.).

**1. What are we to praise God for?**
(We are to praise God for all He is and for the great things He does.)

**2. What are we to use to praise God?**
(We are to use all that we know of and have available to us.)

**3. In what situations are we to praise God?**
(We are to praise God in every situation and circumstance.)

**4. In what settings are we to praise God?**
(We are to praise wherever we are, wherever we may be.)

**5. What other guidelines does this Scripture give for praising God?**

**6. Does contemporary Christian music meet these guidelines? Why or why not?**
(There is something very attractive and enticing about many evil desires.)

## SO WHAT?

**What new thing did you learn about contemporary Christian music? How can you make it a part of your life?**

## THINGS TO THINK ABOUT (OPTIONAL)

- Use the questions on page 165 after or as a part of "In the Word."

**1. If you could meet any Christian or secular musician who would it be and why?**

**2. In what ways are Christian musicians different from secular musicians? In what ways are they the same?**

**3. Could contemporary Christian music ever be a negative influence? If so, in what way?**

Fold

# WARM UP

## TIME IS ON MY SIDE

**1.** When I have time to myself I like to...

...........................................................................

...........................................................................

...........................................................................

**2.** When I have time with just one special friend I like to...

...........................................................................

...........................................................................

...........................................................................

**3.** When I'm hanging out with the group I like to...

...........................................................................

...........................................................................

# TEAM EFFORT

## CONTEMPORARY CHRISTIAN MUSIC DIET

List your top five Christian musicians or groups and then fill in the information below.

**Top Five Christian Musicians**

| Name | Style of Music | Favorite Song |
|------|----------------|---------------|
| 1. | | |
| 2. | | |
| 3. | | |
| 4. | | |
| 5. | | |

# In the Word

## PRAISE HIM WITH THE SYNTHESIZER

Read Psalm 150. Now think about the world you live in
(the different types of people, places, things, situations, etc.).

**1.** What are we to praise God for? .................................................................................

.........................................................................................................................................

.........................................................................................................................................

.........................................................................................................................................

**2.** What are we to use to praise God? .................................................................  .......

.........................................................................................................................................

.........................................................................................................................................

.........................................................................................................................................

**3.** In what situations are we to praise God? .......................................................................

.........................................................................................................................................

.........................................................................................................................................

.........................................................................................................................................

**4.** In what settings are we to praise God? ...........................................................................

.........................................................................................................................................

.........................................................................................................................................

**5.** What other guidelines does this Scripture give for praising God? .....................................

.........................................................................................................................................

.........................................................................................................................................

.........................................................................................................................................

**6.** Does contemporary Christian music meet these guidelines? Why or why not? ...................

.........................................................................................................................................

.........................................................................................................................................

.........................................................................................................................................

.........................................................................................................................................

## So What?

What new thing did you learn about contemporary Christian music? How can you
make it a part of your life?

.....................................................................  .  .............

.........................................................................................

.........................................................................................

.........................................................................................

.........................................................................................

.........................................................................................

.........................................................................................

# Things to Think About

**1.** If you could meet any Christian or secular musician who would it be and why?

.................................................................................................................................

.................................................................................................................................

.................................................................................................................................

**2.** In what ways are Christian musicians different than secular musicians?
In what ways are they the same?

.................................................................................................................................

.................................................................................................................................

.................................................................................................................................

**3.** Could contemporary Christian music ever be a negative influence? If so, in what ways?

.................................................................................................................................

.................................................................................................................................

.................................................................................................................................

.................................................................................................................................

.................................................................................................................................

# PARENT PAGE

## AGREE/DISAGREE/UNSURE

Fill in the word (Agree, Disagree, Unsure) that comes closest to your feeling and thoughts.

**Parent**          **Teen**

........................................................................ I love the music at our church.

........................................................................ Any kind of contemporary Christian music is fine.

........................................................................ Contemporary Christian music is a poor substitute for good secular music.

........................................................................ I'm concerned about the music on top 40 radio.

........................................................................ The lyrics in songs have little or no influence on my actions.

........................................................................ Our family totally disagrees on our views of music.

........................................................................ Psalm 150 is an example of why contemporary Christian music is a good idea.

**Session 11 "Contemporary Christian Music" Date**................................

# DISCRETIONARY VIEWING

## EY VERSE

"Turn my eyes away from worthless things; preserve my life according to your word." Psalm 119:37

## IBLICAL BASIS

Psalm 101:3; 119:37

## THE BIG IDEA

Young people need to be selective in viewing movies and TV programs.

## AIMS OF THIS SESSION

During this session you will guide students to:

- Examine the choices they make in watching TV programs and movies;
- Discover how to discern between biblical and unbiblical TV programs and movies;
- Develop biblical guidelines for watching TV programs and movies.

## WARM UP

**All-time Favorites—**
A listing of favorite movies and TV programs.

## TEAM EFFORT— JUNIOR HIGH/ MIDDLE SCHOOL

**Movie Rating Guide—**
An evaluation of students' favorite movies.

## TEAM EFFORT— HIGH SCHOOL

**The Double Date—**
A story on choices young people have in viewing movies.

## IN THE WORD

**Is It Worth Your While?—**
A Bible study of what is worth watching.

## THINGS TO THINK ABOUT (OPTIONAL)

Questions to get teens thinking and talking about current TV programs and movies.

## PARENT PAGE

A tool to get the session into the home and allow parents and teens to discuss the family TV and movie viewing habits.

## LEADER'S DEVOTIONAL

We all know young people who complain of having nothing to do because they've been trained to think that entertainment, not contribution, is their domain. Bored students get into trouble; drugs and alcohol are the quickest and easiest fix for boredom. They might not buy guns and shoot up their schoolmates, but if one picture is worth a thousand words and we see as much violence as pundits tell us we do, then it certainly is only the grace of God that keeps any of us from shooting everyone we know!

There's an interesting passage in Isaiah 33:4-17 which describes the person who can stand up during a time of judgment in Israel. This person is described as one who walks righteously, but also as one "who stops his ears against plots of murder and shuts his eyes against contemplating evil." Imagine the effect that rule alone would have on our film and TV program selection! We so often think that what we see won't affect us because "it's not real." But do our minds know that? Can enough watching of others' demeaning, cruel, violent actions finally convince us that this behavior is acceptable? Ask your teens some questions that will reveal their attitudes toward other people. What about people who hurt them? Who hurt their friends? Listen for the subtle attitude shifts that indicate that they have bought into the philosophies put forth on film. Like it or not, these people are modeling behavior for all of us. And as we learned earlier, modeling is the most powerful kind of teaching possible.

Maybe it's an outrageous idea, but how about each of us grown-ups taking a *media* purity pledge? Would that cramp our styles too much, make us feel a little too far removed from "the real world"? Perhaps. But unless we begin by *our* modeling to show students that what they are seeing on the big or small screen is less exciting than the real life God has for us, we're just talking. And remember that just *one* picture is worth a thousand words. (Mary Gross, editor, Gospel Light.)

**"Lesbians. Homosexuals. Transvestites. Spiritualists. Occultists. Teenage runaways. Teenage drug addicts. Teenage alcoholics. Child stars who are in trouble."—**

Woman listing people she has met through TV, *The Washington Post Magazine*, January 1, 1994

SESSION TWELVE

BIBLE TUCK-IN™

# DISCRETIONARY VIEWING

## 🔑 KEY VERSE

"Turn my eyes away from worthless things; preserve my life according to your word." Psalm 119:37

## 📖 BIBLICAL BASIS

Psalm 101:3; 119:37

## 📺 THE BIG IDEA

The media is one of the most powerful influences in our life. We can learn to be a selective viewer.

## 🔥 WARM UP (10-15 MINUTES)

### All-time Favorites

- Display a copy of "All-time Favorites" on page 173 using an overhead projector.
- As a whole group, develop a list.

Develop a list of the top 10 movies and TV programs of all time.

Top 10

| Movies | TV programs |
|--------|-------------|
| 1. | |
| 2. | |
| 3. | |
| 4. | |
| 5. | |
| 6. | |
| 7. | |
| 8. | |
| 9. | |
| 10. | |

------- Fold -------

---

2. Read Psalm 119:37. How do we determine what is worthwhile and what is worthless?

3. With these Scriptures in mind complete the lists.

TV programs and movies I will watch:
1.
2.
3.
4.
5.

What in these programs is worthwhile?

TV programs and movies I will not watch:
1.
2.
3.
4.
5.

## 🤔 SO WHAT?

Five principles I will use in viewing TV programs and movies:
1.
2.
3.
4.
5.

## 💭 THINGS TO THINK ABOUT (OPTIONAL)

• Use the questions on page 181 after or as a part of "In the Word."

1. What ingredients make a good movie or a TV program?

2. What's your opinion of the movie rating system (G, PG, PG-13, R, NC17)?

3. What movies or TV programs have you seen recently that would be most Christ honoring? What recent movies or TV programs are the least Christ honoring?

## 📄 PARENT PAGE

• Distribute page to parents.

DISCRETIONARY VIEWING

# TEAM EFFORT—JUNIOR HIGH/MIDDLE SCHOOL (15-20 MINUTES)

## MOVIE RATING GUIDE

- Divide students into pairs.
- Give each student a copy of "Movie Rating Guide" on page 175 and a pen or pencil.
- Students rate their favorite movies.

Complete this rating sheet for several of your favorite movies.

**My favorite movies**

1. ...................................................
2. ...................................................
3. ...................................................
4. ...................................................
5. ...................................................

Score each movie in the following categories from 1 (very positive) to 10 (very negative). Write DA if the category doesn't apply.

| | | | | | |
|---|---|---|---|---|---|
| Language | 1. | 2. | 3. | 4. | 5. |
| Violence | 1. | 2. | 3. | 4. | 5. |
| Sensuality | 1. | 2. | 3. | 4. | 5. |
| Serious issues | 1. | 2. | 3. | 4. | 5. |
| Use of humor | 1. | 2. | 3. | 4. | 5. |
| Healthy morals and values | 1. | 2. | 3. | 4. | 5. |

# TEAM EFFORT—HIGH SCHOOL (15-20 MINUTES)

## THE DOUBLE DATE

- Divide students into groups of three or four.
- Give each student a copy of "The Double Date" on page 177 and a pen or pencil, or display the page using an overhead projector.
- Students read story and answer questions.
- As a whole group, discuss questions.

Ron and Pam went on their first double date with another couple from the church youth group. They were looking forward to a great evening and told their parents the plan was to go out to McDonald's (big spenders!) and then to the latest G-rated Disney movie.

After a fun time at McDonald's, they arrived at the theater only to notice that another movie playing was the hot new film "Tonight's the Night." This movie was rated R and the advertisement said extreme use of sex, violence and harsh language. The other couple said, "Tonight's the Night' looks great. Let's see it. The Disney movie looks like it's for little kids." Ron and Pam didn't know what to do. They had told their parents they were going to watch the Disney movie and both sets of parents usually did not allow them to see R-rated films.

1. What are Ron and Pam's options?

2. What could happen to Ron and Pam's friendship with the other couple?

3. What if Ron wanted to go to the R-rated film and Pam didn't want to go?

4. Do their parents need to know every movie they see?

5. How should they choose the movie they will view?

# ON THE WORD (25-33 MINUTES)

## IS IT WORTH YOUR WHILE?

- Give each student a copy of "Is It Worth Your While?" on page 179 and a pen or pencil.
- As a whole group, complete the Bible study.
- Students individually complete lists.

1. Read Psalm 101:3. How can we keep our eyes from vile things?

# WARM UP

## ALL-TIME FAVORITES

Develop a list of the top 10 movies and TV programs of all time.

### Top 10

| Movies | TV programs |
|---|---|
| **1.** | |
| **2.** | |
| **3.** | |
| **4.** | |
| **5.** | |
| **6.** | |
| **7.** | |
| **8.** | |
| **9.** | |
| **10.** | |

# TEAM EFFORT

## MOVIE RATING GUIDE

Complete this rating sheet for several of your favorite movies.

**Favorite movies**

1. ........................................................................................
2. ........................................................................................
3. ........................................................................................
4. ........................................................................................
5. ........................................................................................

Score each movie in the following categories from 1 (very positive) to 10 (very negative). Write DA if the category doesn't apply.

| | | | | | |
|---|---|---|---|---|---|
| **Language** | 1. | 2. | 3. | 4. | 5. |
| **Violence** | 1. | 2. | 3. | 4. | 5. |
| **Sexuality** | 1. | 2. | 3. | 4. | 5. |
| **Serious issues** | 1. | 2. | 3. | 4. | 5. |
| **Use of humor** | 1. | 2. | 3. | 4. | 5. |
| **Healthy morals and values** | 1. | 2. | 3. | 4. | 5. |

# EAM EFFORT

## THE DOUBLE DATE

Ron and Pam went on their first double date with another couple from the church youth group. They were looking forward to a great evening and told their parents the plan was to go out to McDonald's (big spenders!) and then to the latest G-rated Disney movie.

After a fun time at McDonald's, they arrived at the theater only to notice that another movie playing was the hot new film "Tonight's the Night." This movie was rated R and the advertisement said extreme use of sex, violence and harsh language. The other couple said, "'Tonight's the Night' looks great. Let's see it. The Disney movie looks like it's for little kids." Ron and Pam didn't know what to do. They had told their parents they were going to watch the Disney movie and both sets of parents usually did not allow them to see R-rated films.

**1. What are Ron and Pam's options?**

.................................................. ..................................................

..................................................................................................

..................................................................................................

**2. What could happen to Ron and Pam's friendship with the other couple?**

..................................................................................................

..................................................................................................

..................................................................................................

**3. What if Ron wanted to go to the R-rated film and Pam didn't want to go?**

..................................................................................................

..................................................................................................

..................................................................................................

**4. Do their parents need to know every movie they see?**

..................................................................................................

..................................................................................................

..................................................................................................

..................................................................................................

**5. How should they choose the movie they will view?**

..................................................................................................

..................................................................................................

..................................................................................................

..................................................................................................

# IN THE WORD

## IS IT WORTH YOUR WHILE?

**1.** Read Psalm 101:3. How can we keep our eyes from vile things?

.................................................................................................

.................................................................................................

.................................................................................................

**2.** Read Psalm 119:37. How do we determine what is worthwhile and what is worthless?

.................................................................................................

.................................................................................................

**3.** With these Scriptures in mind complete the lists.

TV programs and movies I will watch:

1. ...............................................................................................

2. ...............................................................................................

3. ...............................................................................................

4. ...............................................................................................

5. ...............................................................................................

What in these programs is worthwhile?

TV programs and movies I will not watch:

1. ...............................................................................................

2. ...............................................................................................

3. ...............................................................................................

4. ...............................................................................................

5. ...............................................................................................

# SO WHAT?

Five principles I will use in viewing TV programs and movies:

1. ...............................................................................................

2. ...............................................................................................

3. ...............................................................................................

4. ...............................................................................................

# THINGS TO THINK ABOUT

**1.** What ingredients make a good movie or a TV program? ........................................................
...................................................................................................................................
...................................................................................................................................
...................................................................................................................................

**2.** What's your opinion of the movie rating system (G, PG, PG-13, R, NC17)? ........................
...................................................................................................................................
...................................................................................................................................
...................................................................................................................................

**3.** What movies or TV programs have you seen recently that would be most Christ honoring?
What recent movies or TV programs are the least Christ honoring? ......................................
...................................................................................................................................
...................................................................................................................................
...................................................................................................................................

# PARENT PAGE

**1.** Does our family have a tele-holic attitude about our TV? ...................................................................

....................................................................................................................................................................

....................................................................................................................................................................

....................................................................................................................................................................

**2.** Has TV or movies gotten in the way of family communication in the past month? ........................................

....................................................................................................................................................................

....................................................................................................................................................................

....................................................................................................................................................................

**3.** What bugs you most about TV? ...................................................................................................................

....................................................................................................................................................................

....................................................................................................................................................................

....................................................................................................................................................................

**4.** What do you like best about TV? ...............................................................................................................

....................................................................................................................................................................

....................................................................................................................................................................

## TV/MOVIE VIEWING CONTRACT

1. The average amount of hours the TV can be on in our home per day is ...........................

2. The movie ratings that are available for each family member to view are ...........................

3. The TV programs that are not acceptable in our home are ...........................

4. The family agreement about MTV is ...........................

5. A TV program that could be a fun family weekly date is ...........................

6. A movie that fits biblical standards that we could watch as a family is ...........................

**Session 12 "Discretionary Viewing" Date** ...........................

# PRAISE FOR YOUTHBUILDERS

continued from page 6

In *YouthBuilders Group Bible Studies*, Jim Burns pulls together the key ingredients for an effective curriculum series. Jim captures the combination of teen involvement, and a solid biblical perspective, with topics that are relevant and straightforward. This series will be a valuable tool in the local church.
**Dennis "Tiger" McLuen,** Executive Director, Youth Leadership

My ministry takes me to the lost kids in our nation's cities where youth games and activities are often irrelevant and plain Bible knowledge for the sake of learning is unattractive. Young people need the information necessary to make wise decisions related to everyday problems. *YouthBuilders* will help many young people integrate their faith into everyday life, which after all is our goal as youth workers.
**Miles McPherson,** President, Project Intercept

Finally, a Bible study that has it all! It's action-packed, practical and biblical; but that's only the beginning. *YouthBuilders* involves students in the Scriptures. It's relational, interactive and leads kids towards lifestyle changes. The unique aspect is a page for parents, something that's usually missing from adolescent curriculum. Jim Burns has outdone himself. This isn't a homerun—it's a grandslam!
**Dr. David Olshine,** Director of Youth Ministries, Columbia International University

Here is a thoughtful and relevant curriculum designed to meet the needs of youth workers, parents and students. It's creative, interactive and biblical—and with Jim Burns' name on it, you know you're getting a quality resource.
**Laurie Polich,** Youth Director, First Presbyterian Church of Berkeley

Jim Burns has done a fantastic job of putting together a youth curriculum that will work. *YouthBuilders* provides the motivation and information for leaders and the types of experience and content that will capture junior high and high school people. I recommend it highly.
**Denny Rydberg,** President, Young Life

In 10 years of youth ministry I've never used a curriculum because I've never found anything that actively involves students in the learning process, speaks to young people where they are and challenges them with biblical truth—I'll use this! *YouthBuilders Group Bible Studies* is a complete curriculum that is helpful to parents, youth leaders and, most importantly, today's youth.
**Glenn Schroeder,** Youth and Young Adult Ministries, Vineyard Christian Fellowship, Anaheim

185

This new material by Jim Burns represents a vitality in curriculum and, I believe, a more mature and faithful direction. *YouthBuilders Group Bible Studies* challenges youth by teaching them how to make decisions rather than telling them what decisions to make. Each session offers teaching concepts, presents options and asks for a decision. I believe it's healthy, the way Christ taught and represents the abilities, personhood and faithfulness of youth. I give it an A+!
**J. David Stone,** President,
Stone & Associates

Jim Burns has done it again! This is a practical, timely and reality-based resource for equipping teens to live life in the fast-paced, pressure-packed adolescent world of the 90s. A very refreshing creative oasis in the curriculum desert!
**Rich Van Pelt,** President,
Alongside Ministries

# How to Outlive Your Youth Group

We realize that your highest goal in life may not be to become the world's oldest, and wisest, youth worker. But if it was, these are the resources to get you there.

## Keep your group on the right track with YouthBuilders.

Bringing the gospel to young people doesn't have to be a hit-or-miss affair. **YouthBuilders Group Bible Studies** are high-involvement, discussion-oriented, and Bible-centered approaches to youth curriculum. Each **YouthBuilders Bible Study** is modular to suit your needs, as well as comprehensive to see your young people through their high school years. Stay on the right track with **YouthBuilders.**

**Look for these issues in coming volumes of YouthBuilders—**
#2 Prayer, Developing a Devotional Life
#3 Next Step for New Believers, Christian Basics
#4 Peer Leadership, Spiritual Gifts and Sharing Your Faith
#5 Servanthood, Commitment, Discipleship
#6 Crisis Issues and Peer Counseling

**Jim Burns**

---

## More Youth Worker Resources

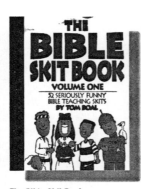

**The Bible Skit Book**
Tom Boal
Get your kids out of their seats and into the Word. Fifty-two lively, reproducible Bible-theme skits for all ages. Each skit includes director's tips, Bible background info and group discussion questions.
Manual • ISBN 08307.16238 • $16.99
Also available More Bible Skits
Manual • ISBN 08307.16238 • $16.99

**Super Clip Art for Youth Workers—On Disk**
Tom Finley
Illustrations, cartoons, borders and more in a format you can use on your computer. Compatible with most software. Includes 3.5-inch disks, user's instructions and a paperback copy of Super Clip Art for Youth Workers.
IBM 3.5-inch disks
SPCN 25116.06670 • $39.99
Macintosh 3.5-inch disks
SPCN 25116.06593 • $39.99

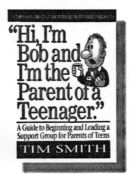

**Hi, I'm Bob and I'm the Parent of a Teenager**
Tim Smith
This seven-session course focuses on biblical principles of parenting and explains seven building blocks to becoming an effective parent. Designed to help youth ministers launch peer-lead parent support groups.
Manual • ISBN 08307.14650 • $14.99

**The Youth Worker's Emergency Manual**
A collection of "instant" Bible studies, action games, surveys and a host of other activities. It's the perfect cure for emergencies like a cancellation from your speaker, lost lesson notes or a flat tire on a youth bus.
Manual • ISBN 08307.14677 • $8.99

**Youth Worker's Book of Case Studies**
Jim Burns
Fifty true case studies, compiled by Jim Burns, pose real-life moral questions to teenagers for group discussion and learning. Scripture references and discussion questions included.
Manual • ISBN 08307.15827 • $9.99

**Gospel Light**

**Ask your local Christian supplier for these and other Gospel Light resources to build your youth group.**